Beyond The Nest How Birds Communicate In The Wild

By
Olivia K

INDEX Page Nos

INTRODUCTION

"Past the Home: How Birds Convey in Nature" unfurls as a significant investigation into the mind boggling and enamoring universe of avian correspondence, rising above the limits of homes and enclosures to dive into the actual pith of wild bird exchanges. In this extensive excursion, we leave on a journey to translate the bunch manners by which birds speak, opening the mysteries implanted in their calls, tunes, and ways of behaving that reverberation through the untamed scenes they call home.

I. Prelude to the Avian Orchestra
The Advancement of Understanding

Our process initiates with a review look into the development of avian correspondence studies. From the beginning of ornithology to the contemporary time of refined research strategies, we explore the scholarly scenes formed by the persistent pursuit to understand the complicated dialects of our padded associates. The story unfurls against the scenery of verifiable forward leaps and logical achievements, preparing for a top to bottom investigation of the nuanced correspondence frameworks that oversee avian communications in nature.

The Variety of Avian Life

As we step into the domain of wild bird correspondence, we are faced with the stunning variety of avian life. Every species, whether taking off high overhead or scrounging on the backwoods floor, contributes an interesting rhythm to the ensemble of nature. The story, similar to an all encompassing focal point, focuses in on the changed territories and biological systems that shape avian correspondence, making way for a vivid investigation of the multi-layered manners by which birds articulate their thoughts past the bounds of their homes.

II. The Language of Flight
Relocation Examples and Aeronautical Discussions

The principal section takes off, straightforwardly, as we investigate the language of flight and the significant messages woven into the transient examples of birds. From the Cold tern's awe-inspiring excursions across halves of the globe to the synchronized arrangements of geese, we disentangle the airborne discussions that guide runs through tremendous scopes. It is an entrancing look into the cooperative route and correspondence systems that empower these winged migrants to navigate landmasses and oppose geographic limits.

Connections in Mid-Air

Our excursion through the ethereal domain stretches out past relocation, diving into the collaborations that unfold during flight. Whether participated in stunning romance shows or synchronized ethereal tumbling, birds convey not exclusively to explore yet additionally to lay out friendly securities and build up the perplexing embroidered artwork of their networks. From a perspective of ethology and environmental setting, we interpret the meaning of these mid-air exchanges that unfurl against the material of the open sky.

III. Grounded Discussions
Settling Ways of behaving and Parental Correspondence

Diving from the skies, we enter the close space of grounded discussions. In this part, we examine the ways of behaving related with settling, from the fastidious development of homes to the cooperative endeavors of nurturing. It is a nuanced investigation of how avian guardians speak with their posterity, utilizing a collection of vocalizations and signals to guarantee the endurance and prosperity of the future. From the perspective of ethology and transformative science, we disentangle the versatile meaning of these grounded discoursed.

Calls for An area and Guard

The account then moves to the regional calls and safeguard instruments that characterize the ground-level talk among birds. From the unpleasant calls of the crackpot on a peaceful lake to the boisterous bedlam of shorebirds guarding their taking care of grounds, we analyze the vocalizations that act as statements of proprietorship and admonitions of expected dangers. The section tests the unpredictable harmony among rivalry and collaboration in the unique auditorium of regional correspondence.

IV. Past Tune: The Songs of Nature
Top to bottom Examination of Bird Tunes

With a musical crescendo, we dive into the melodic domain of bird tunes, a foundation of avian correspondence. Section by part, we investigate the complexities of avian vocalizations, from the heartfelt tunes of warblers to the musical drumming of woodpeckers on thunderous tree trunks. From a perspective of acoustic biology and conduct nature, we decipher the secret messages implanted in the differed and charming tunes that resound through timberlands, knolls, and mountains.

Connection among Melodies and Regenerative Way of behaving

The investigation of bird melodies stretches out past their tasteful appeal, unwinding their significant job in regenerative ways of behaving.

The part inspects how these vocalizations act as romance ceremonies, signs of fruitfulness, and markers of hereditary wellness. From transformative perspectives, we perceive the versatile meaning of many-sided tunes that have advanced over centuries to pass on magnificence as well as urgent data about the regenerative wellness of their arrangers.

Provincial Varieties in Birdsong

The orchestra of bird melodies traverses mainlands, yet territorial varieties add a rich layer to our investigation. Whether the mimicry of lyrebirds in the Australian rainforests or the eerie calls of crackpots in North American lakes, we disentangle the geological subtleties that shape avian vocalizations. This section fills in as a diverse excursion, featuring the exceptional vernaculars and territorial varieties that add to the worldwide embroidery of bird correspondence.

V. Visual Signals and Non-verbal communication
Romance Shows and Mating Ceremonies

Past vocalizations, avian correspondence envelops a visual language communicated through romance shows and mating ceremonies. In this part, we witness the astonishing cluster of motions, moves, and shows that birds utilize to draw in mates and lay out pair bonds. From the flashy plumage presentations of birds of heaven to the synchronized romance trips of raptors, we unravel the quiet exchanges that unfurl through visual signs chasing regenerative achievement.

Non-vocal Specialized Strategies

The story widens its degree to investigate the assorted range of non-vocal specialized strategies utilized by birds. Through a multicolored focal point, we witness the unobtrusive language passed on through body stances, feather shows, and material connections. Whether participated in multifaceted romance moves or passing alerts on through unobtrusive developments, birds explore the complexities of their social world through a quiet yet smooth collection of non-vocal articulations.

Job of Plumage and Motions in Avian Communication

Plumage turns into a material of articulation as we dive into the job of quills and non-verbal communication in avian collaborations. From obscure shading for disguise to lively presentations for romance, plumage fills in as a unique medium through which birds impart their personality, wellbeing, and conceptive status. This part uncovers the obvious signs implanted in quills and signals, representing how they capability as a visual dictionary in the great story of avian correspondence.

VI. The Mysterious Existence of Bird Calls
Mysterious Correspondence and Caution Calls

A cloak of secret wraps the universe of bird calls, and in this section, we disentangle the mysterious life implanted in these apparently straightforward expressions. From mysterious correspondence that disguises the presence of hunters to the criticalness passed on through alert calls, we peer into the secret layers of avian vocalizations. It is an excursion into the stealthy universe of short and deliberate calls that encode data urgent for the endurance of people and networks.

Secret Messages in Short and Straightforward Calls

Expanding upon the establishment laid in the past section, we further investigate the secret messages hid inside short and apparently clear calls. The story uncovers the intricacy underneath straightforwardness, uncovering how succinct vocalizations pass on an abundance of data about food accessibility, ecological circumstances, and social elements. Through acoustic investigation and field perceptions, we analyze the language of compact calls that accentuate the sonic scene of nature.

Concentrating on Bird Discussions in Nature

The investigation of bird calls stretches out past individual expressions, welcoming us to observe the unique discussions that unfurl inside avian networks. Specialists outfitted with refined recording gear and insightful apparatuses snoop on the unpredictable exchanges that shape the social texture of bird social orders. Through field studies and bioacoustic examinations, we gain experiences into the public idea of avian correspondence and the job it plays in molding agreeable ways of behaving and social orders.

VII. The Job of Climate in Correspondence
Impact of Environment on Correspondence Styles

The regular world isn't just a scenery however a functioning member in the show of avian correspondence. In this part, we investigate how various natural surroundings and biological systems shape the correspondence styles of occupant birds. From the thick shelters of rainforests to the extensive deserts, every climate forces its remarkable difficulties and open doors, encouraging the development of unmistakable vocalizations and correspondence procedures.

Variations in Correspondence to Natural Difficulties

Expanding upon the investigation of living space impact, we dig into the versatile methodologies that birds utilize to conquer ecological difficulties. Whether exploring the hear-able intricacies of thick vegetation or imparting across immense open spreads, birds grandstand striking transformations in their vocalizations and ways of behaving.

This section unfurls as a demonstration of the strength and creativity of avian correspondence notwithstanding different and dynamic biological scenes.

Effect of Environment and Occasional Changes on Bird Correspondence
The cadence of avian correspondence is complicatedly sensitive to the patterns of environment and occasional changes. From the rich ensembles of spring to the stifled discoursed of winter, we investigate how birds adjust their correspondence designs because of natural vacillations. An occasional excursion unwinds the effect of environmental change on the fleeting elements of avian correspondence, featuring the weakness of these sensitive frameworks notwithstanding an influencing world.

VIII. Human-Prompted Changes in Avian Correspondence
Impacts of Urbanization on Bird Correspondence
As our investigation reaches out to the effect of human exercises, we stand up to the significant impacts of urbanization on avian correspondence. The change of regular scenes into metropolitan conditions presents a chaos of anthropogenic sounds, disturbing the acoustic scenes that birds depend upon for correspondence. Through contextual analyses and natural examinations, we look at the difficulties presented by urbanization and the versatile techniques utilized by birds in exploring these changed sonic conditions.

Clamor Contamination and its Effect on Vocalization
The story then, at that point, focuses on the particular danger of commotion contamination, an unavoidable result of human exercises that saturates both metropolitan and regular spaces. From the tenacious murmur of traffic to modern clatter, we investigate how raised commotion levels slow down avian vocalizations, upsetting basic correspondence capabilities. Through trial studies and field perceptions, we disclose the inconspicuous yet broad results of commotion contamination on the acoustic texture of bird correspondence.

Preservation Suggestions for Wild Bird Correspondence
The investigation of human-prompted changes in avian correspondence finishes in an assessment of the preservation suggestions. As wild spaces reduce and human impact extends, the fragile equilibrium of avian correspondence faces remarkable difficulties. The story turns into a source of inspiration, encouraging perusers to think about the interconnectedness of bird correspondence and biodiversity preservation. It is an investigation of how understanding and relieving the effects of human exercises can shield the complex dialects that have developed over centuries.

IX. Mechanical Advances in Concentrating on Avian Correspondence
Outline of Present day Exploration Methods
With a change in center, the story unfurls to grandstand the mechanical wonders that have upset the investigation of avian correspondence. From the unassuming recording device to refined bioacoustics apparatuses, we follow the advancement of exploration procedures that permit researchers to listen in on the confidential discussions of birds. This section fills in as an exhaustive outline of the stockpile of advancements that empower phenomenal experiences into the universe of avian correspondence.

Progressions in Bioacoustics and Following Advancements
The investigation of mechanical advances extends as we spotlight the particular forward leaps in bioacoustics and following advancements. Scientists furnished with directional mouthpieces, robotized sound acknowledgment programming, and GPS beacons dig into the complicated subtleties of bird vocalizations and developments. Through contextual analyses and mechanical profiles, we uncover the extraordinary force of these advancements in unwinding the secrets of avian correspondence.

Bits of knowledge Acquired from Mechanical Advancements
The account finishes in an investigation of the significant bits of knowledge acquired from these mechanical advancements. From interpreting the importance behind complex melody groupings to following the transitory courses of subtle species, scientists outfit the force of innovation to push the limits of avian correspondence studies. It is a festival of how these devices have extended our comprehension, giving a nuanced and point by point picture of the correspondence frameworks that support the existences of birds in nature.

A.   Overview of Bird Communication
Birds, with their assorted plumage, resonant tunes, and perplexing ways of behaving, have long spellbound human creative mind. However, past their stylish allure, these padded occupants of the skies take part in a modern type of correspondence that is both multifaceted and vital for their endurance. This investigation sets out on an outline of bird correspondence, disentangling the diverse manners by which our avian partners pass on data, lay out friendly bonds, and explore the intricacies of their surroundings.

I. The Authentic Woven artwork of Avian Correspondence Studies
Early Perceptions and Ornithological Trailblazers
The underlying foundations of avian correspondence studies expand profound into history, with early naturalists and ornithologists mentioning fundamental objective facts.

From Aristotle's considerations on bird conduct to the fastidious notes of John James Audubon, the authentic embroidered artwork is woven with strings of interest and sharp perception. This part dives into the commitments of trailblazers who laid the basis for current investigations, exhibiting the development of how we might interpret bird correspondence.

From Field Notes to Contemporary Exploration
The excursion from hand-attracted delineations to contemporary exploration strategies is set apart by a progression of leap forwards. The approach of optics, sound recording gadgets, and, all the more as of late, trend setting innovations like bioacoustics and GPS following, has reformed the investigation of bird correspondence. This segment gives an outline of the advancement of examination systems, featuring the vital minutes that moved our investigation into the many-sided universe of avian language.

II. Scientific classification of Avian Vocalizations
Calls, Tunes, and Then some
Avian correspondence appears in different vocalizations, each serving unmistakable capabilities. Calls, frequently short and straightforward, pass on prompt data and are basic for endurance. Melodies, then again, are more intricate and normally connected with romance and regional showcases. This segment takes apart the scientific classification of avian vocalizations, revealing insight into the nuanced qualifications among calls and tunes and the heap manners by which birds use these vocal apparatuses.

Contact Calls and Alert Calls
The range of calls envelops contact calls, effectively keeping up with bunch union, and alert calls, flagging risk and preparing aggregate reactions. From a perspective of conduct nature, this subsection investigates the versatile meaning of various call types, unwinding the complexities of avian correspondence with regards to differed ecological difficulties and social elements.

III. The Visual Language: Plumage, Motions, and Shows
Plumage as a Material of Correspondence
While vocalizations become the overwhelming focus, the visual language of birds is similarly dazzling. Plumage, with its different tones, examples, and designs, fills in as a powerful material of correspondence. From obscure shading for cover to lively showcases for romance, this segment explores the obvious prompts implanted in feathers, disentangling the rich woven artwork of avian correspondence communicated through the language of plumage.

Romance Shows and Mating Customs

Past quills, romance shows and mating customs comprise an outwardly breathtaking part of avian correspondence. Elaborate moves, mind boggling flights, and shows of plumage are organized to draw in mates and lay out pair securities. Through social biology and ethological focal points, we investigate the job of visual signs in the complicated movement of romance customs, revealing insight into the transformative meaning of these showcases.

IV. Past Homes: Avian Correspondence Across Living spaces
Variations to Different Conditions

Birds occupy a variety of biological systems, from thick rainforests to dry deserts, each monumental extraordinary difficulties on correspondence. This segment digs into how avian correspondence adjusts to assorted living spaces. From the sharp calls of woods birds exploring through thick foliage to the conveying melodies of open-country species, we investigate the striking variations that permit birds to impart successfully in their particular surroundings.

Natural Effects on Correspondence Styles

The impact of environment stretches out past transformations to the actual attributes of vocalizations. Ecological elements shape correspondence styles, impacting the recurrence, term, and intricacy of avian vocalizations. This subsection inspects the multifaceted exchange among birds and their living spaces, disentangling how the acoustic scene and underlying highlights of the climate shape the language of quills and sound.

V. The Social Embroidered artwork of Bird Melodies
Provincial Varieties and Lingos

Bird melodies reverberation across landmasses, making a worldwide orchestra with territorial varieties and lingos. This segment leaves on a social investigation of bird tunes, unwinding the geological subtleties that shape avian vocalizations. From the mimicry of lyrebirds in Australian rainforests to the assorted vernaculars of melody sparrows in North America, we dive into the rich woven artwork of territorial varieties that add to the worldwide vocabulary of bird correspondence.

Human Discernments and Social Importance

Bird melodies have penetrated human culture, impacting legends, writing, and workmanship. This subsection investigates the convergence between human insights and avian vocalizations.

From the emblematic implications ascribed to explicit bird tunes to the creative motivation drawn from their songs, we disentangle the social meaning of bird correspondence, delineating how these padded choristers have made a permanent imprint on the human creative mind.

VI. The Mysterious Language of Bird Calls
Secretive Correspondence and Short Calls
Inside the complicated snare of bird calls lies a secret language of enigmatic correspondence and short, deliberate calls. This part uncovers the mysterious life implanted in apparently basic vocalizations. From calls that cover the presence of hunters to succinct signs that pass on data about food accessibility, we dig into the unpretentious and frequently ignored parts of avian correspondence.

Public Discussions and Social Elements
The story reaches out past individual calls to investigate the shared discussions that shape avian social elements. Birds take part in complex trades, utilizing calls to facilitate bunch developments, signal the revelation of assets, and lay out friendly pecking orders. Through a blend of field studies and bioacoustic investigations, we gain experiences into the unpredictable discoursed that unfurl inside avian networks, enlightening the mutual idea of their language.

VII. Human-Prompted Changes in Avian Correspondence
Urbanization and Adjusted Soundscapes
As human impact extends, wild spaces reduce, and avian correspondence faces remarkable difficulties. This segment looks at the impacts of urbanization on bird correspondence, as normal scenes change into metropolitan conditions portrayed by a clamor of anthropogenic sounds. From the effect on reproducing accomplishment to changed singing ways of behaving, we disentangle the complex manners by which birds explore these changed soundscapes.

Clamor Contamination: Upsetting the Sonic Scene
A particular danger inside the more extensive setting of urbanization is clamor contamination, an unavoidable outcome of human exercises that penetrates both metropolitan and normal spaces. This subsection focuses on how raised commotion levels impede avian vocalizations, upsetting basic correspondence capabilities. Through exploratory investigations and field perceptions, we reveal the unpretentious yet expansive results of commotion contamination on the acoustic texture of bird correspondence.

Protection Suggestions for Avian Correspondence
The investigation of human-actuated changes in avian correspondence finishes in an assessment of protection suggestions. As wild spaces lessen and human impact extends, the sensitive equilibrium of avian correspondence faces phenomenal difficulties. This segment turns into a source of inspiration, encouraging perusers to think about the interconnectedness of bird correspondence and biodiversity protection. It is an investigation of how understanding and relieving the effects of human exercises can defend the perplexing dialects that have developed over centuries.

VIII. Mechanical Wonders: Snoopping on Avian Discussions
Secrets to success: From Optics to Bioacoustics
Mechanical developments have changed the investigation of avian correspondence, permitting specialists to snoop on the confidential discussions of birds. This segment gives an outline of the secrets to success, from the unassuming optics to refined bioacoustics gear. It follows the advancement of innovation that has engaged researchers to unwind the secrets of avian correspondence in extraordinary detail.

Bioacoustics and Computerized Sound Acknowledgment
The story extends as we spotlight explicit mechanical wonders in the domains of bioacoustics and computerized sound acknowledgment. These advancements permit scientists to examine immense measures of acoustic information, opening examples, and implications inside the intricate embroidered artwork of bird vocalizations. Through contextual analyses and mechanical profiles, we reveal the groundbreaking force of these developments in growing comprehension we might interpret avian correspondence.

Experiences Acquired: Translating Tune Groupings and Relocation Courses
The investigation of mechanical advances comes full circle in an assessment of the significant bits of knowledge acquired from these developments. From translating the significance behind complex melody successions to following the transient courses of subtle species, scientists saddle the force of innovation to push the limits of avian correspondence studies. This segment fills in as a festival of how these devices have extended our comprehension, giving a nuanced and itemized representation of the correspondence frameworks that support the existences of birds in nature.

B.   Significance of Studying Avian Communication in the Wild
The investigation of avian correspondence in the wild is an investigation into the core of nature's sonic embroidery, where the melodic ensemble of bird calls, tunes, and visual showcases uncovers a mind boggling and interconnected trap of life.

Understanding the meaning of digging into avian correspondence goes past simple interest; it is a vital aspect for disentangling the insider facts of natural communications, social elements, and the actual texture of biodiversity.

I. Biodiversity and Biological system Elements
Avian Correspondence as a Sign of Environment Wellbeing

One of the central explanations behind concentrating on avian correspondence in the wild lies in its job as a mark of environment wellbeing. Birds are vital parts of biological systems, adding to different environmental cycles, for example, seed dispersal, bug control, and fertilization. By unraveling their correspondence designs, analysts gain experiences into the perplexing connections among birds and their surroundings. Changes in correspondence can flag shifts in biodiversity, helping researchers screen and grasp the strength of environments.

Environmental Collaborations and Conjunction

Avian correspondence is a foundation of environmental collaborations, impacting how species exist together and contend inside a given territory. Concentrating on these communications in the wild uncovers the techniques birds utilize to explore complex biological systems. From laying out regions through vocalizations to planning rummaging exercises, the perplexing dance of avian correspondence portrays the interconnected jobs birds play in supporting the fragile equilibrium of nature.

II. Social Construction and Conduct Biology
Territoriality and Social Ordered progression

In the wild, avian correspondence fills in as a window into the social designs and ordered progressions that oversee bird networks. Through vocalizations and visual showcases, birds pass on data about their personality, societal position, and conceptive wellness. By concentrating on these elements, specialists gain experiences into the perplexing ways of behaving that shape avian social orders, from various leveled structures inside runs to the foundation and protection of regions essential for rearing achievement.

Parental Consideration and Posterity Correspondence

Avian correspondence reaches out past mate fascination and region protection to incorporate significant parts of parental consideration. Concentrating on the connections among guardians and posterity uncovers how correspondence works with the provisioning of food, assurance, and the exchange of fundamental abilities. The importance lies in understanding the complexities of these parent-posterity discoursed, revealing insight into the methodologies birds utilize to guarantee the endurance and progress of the future.

III. Developmental Bits of knowledge and Variations
Advancement of Vocal Collection

Avian correspondence gives a rich embroidery of vocalizations that has developed north of millions of years. By concentrating on the variety and intricacy of bird calls and melodies in the wild, scientists can uncover signs about the developmental history of avian species. This investigation not just disentangles the versatile meaning of explicit vocalizations yet in addition reveals insight into how correspondence procedures have molded the variety of bird species we notice today.

Transformations to Ecological Difficulties

Birds occupy a great many conditions, each introducing extraordinary difficulties to correspondence. From thick timberlands where sound might be suppressed to open scenes where signs can travel significant distances, concentrating on avian correspondence in different territories uncovers the variations birds have created to conquer natural difficulties. These transformations give important bits of knowledge into the coevolutionary connection among birds and their natural surroundings.

IV. Protection and Biodiversity Conservation
Avian Correspondence as a Preservation Device

The investigation of avian correspondence arises as an amazing asset for protection endeavors. Changes in bird correspondence examples can flag biological disturbances, natural surroundings debasement, or the infringement of obtrusive species. Observing these progressions empowers moderates to recognize regions needing insurance, carry out designated preservation methodologies, and survey the adequacy of protection drives over the long run.

Lead Species and Public Commitment

Birds, frequently viewed as lead species, catch public consideration and fondness. Concentrating on avian correspondence in the wild adds to logical information as well as fills in as a vehicle for public commitment to preservation. The charming songs and enthralling presentations of birds can motivate a more profound association with nature, encouraging a feeling of obligation and stewardship for the safeguarding of biodiversity.

V. Innovative Headways and Bioacoustic Checking
Mechanical Advancements in Avian Correspondence Exploration

Ongoing mechanical headways have reformed the field of avian correspondence research. Bioacoustic observing, outfitted with refined recording gadgets and computerized sound acknowledgment programming, permits analysts to gather huge measures of acoustic information in nature.

This innovation empowers the examination of whole soundscapes, offering a far reaching comprehension of avian correspondence designs and adding to enormous scope biodiversity checking endeavors.

Experiences into Conduct Reactions
Mechanical advancements not just upgrade our capacity to record and break down bird vocalizations yet additionally give experiences into the social reactions of birds to different improvements. From the impacts of environmental change on rearing ways of behaving to the effect of human exercises on correspondence designs, bioacoustic checking turns into an incredible asset for concentrating on the unique idea of avian correspondence in light of natural changes.

VI. Moral Contemplations and Preservation Morals
Moral Ramifications of Concentrating on Birds in Nature
While the investigation of avian correspondence in the wild offers important bits of knowledge, it likewise raises moral contemplations. Specialists should explore the harmony between logical request and the prosperity of the concentrated on people and populaces. Moral field rehearses, for example, limiting aggravation and utilizing painless checking methods, become basic to guarantee that the advantages of exploration don't come to the detriment of the government assistance of the concentrated on birds.

Protection Morals and Capable Exploration
Concentrating on avian correspondence in the wild requires a promise to protection morals. Scientists assume a critical part in pushing for the safeguarding of territories, limiting anthropogenic effects, and effectively taking part in endeavors to ration the biological systems that help avian biodiversity. Dependable examination rehearses add to an all encompassing methodology that incorporates logical request with a devotion to the drawn out prosperity of avian populaces and their natural surroundings.

VII. Future Headings and Difficulties
Neglected Domains of Avian Correspondence
In spite of the steps made in understanding avian correspondence, there stay neglected domains and unanswered inquiries. Future examination roads might incorporate a more profound investigation of the mental parts of avian correspondence, the job of individual variety inside species, and the intelligent elements between various correspondence modalities. The continuous improvement of innovation and interdisciplinary joint efforts vows to open new wildernesses in how we might interpret the complexities of avian correspondence.

Challenges in Protection and Exploration Combination
Challenges continue coordinating avian correspondence examination into more extensive preservation drives. Overcoming any barrier between logical information and noteworthy preservation measures requires cooperation between specialists, policymakers, and neighborhood networks. Beating these difficulties includes tending to information holes, imparting discoveries successfully, and encouraging organizations that focus on the conservation of biodiversity and the biological systems that support it.

Chapter 1:
The Language Of Flight

The skies, immense and apparently endless, act as the material whereupon birds paint their stories of movement, route, and elevated correspondence. "The Language of Flight" is an investigation into the many-sided and modern manners by which birds use flight for the purpose of velocity as well as a rich vehicle for correspondence. This extensive excursion will unfurl the assorted parts of avian flight, from the entrancing examples of movement to the unique exchanges that occur mid-air.

I. The Transformative Artful dance of Relocation
A. Verifiable Points of view on Bird Relocation

The peculiarity of bird movement has charmed human interest for a really long time. From antiquated perceptions to contemporary logical comprehension, this part digs into the authentic viewpoints that established the groundwork for our understanding of the transient artful dance. Early naturalists wondered about the occasional developments of birds, and as our insight extended, so did the acknowledgment of movement as a complex versatile system.

B. Exploring Huge Distances: The Hows and Whys of Movement

The incredible excursions of transitory birds range great many kilometers, testing how we might interpret route and direction. Researching the systems behind these relocations, we investigate the job of heavenly prompts, attractive fields, and ecological variables that guide birds across landmasses. The versatile meaning of relocation, from getting to occasional assets to staying away from unforgiving environments, arises as a focal subject in unraveling the language of flight.

C. The Movement of Relocation: Rushing and Arrangement Flying

The language of flight takes on a collective aspect as birds participate in facilitated developments during relocation. Running way of behaving and development flying become parts in the account of avian correspondence. This part analyzes the complexities of these flying showcases, investigating how birds speak with each other to improve productivity, diminish energy use, and explore the difficulties of significant distance flight.

II. Ethereal Discussions: The Elements of Mid-Air Correspondence
A. Romance Showcases overhead

As birds get off the ground, the language of flight reaches out to the domain of romance presentations. From the gymnastic showcases of raptors to the synchronized trips of waterfowl, this part discloses the spellbinding flying exhibitions that assume a vital part in mate choice and match holding. The sky turns into a phase for visual correspondence, with every species contributing its extraordinary movement to the continuous avian ensemble.

B. Tunes and Brings in Flight: The Acoustic Scene of the Skies

Past visual showcases, the language of flight integrates aural aspects. Birds convey through melodies and calls while airborne, adding a layer of intricacy to the orchestra of flight. Examining the acoustic scene of the skies, we investigate how these vocalizations fill needs going from an area guard to keeping in touch inside runs. The transaction among visual and acoustic signs turns into a powerful part of avian correspondence in flight.

III. Grounded Discussions: Settling, Nurturing, and Territoriality
A. Settling Ways of behaving: The Preface to Flight

Prior to taking to the skies, birds participate in grounded discussions related with settling ways of behaving. This segment investigates the language of home development, mate choice, and the complexities of parental correspondence. From intricate romance customs to the helpful endeavors of building homes, the grounded exchanges set up for the aeronautical exhibitions that follow.

B. Parental Correspondence and Nestling Cooperation

When airborne, the language of flight stretches out to the domain of parental consideration. Parental correspondence includes a collection of vocalizations and signals pointed toward guaranteeing the prosperity of posterity. This part investigates the manners by which guardians speak with little birds, from food provisioning to showing fundamental abilities. The elevated viewpoints offer a one of a kind vantage point for understanding the nuanced collaborations among guardians and their young.

C. Regional Calls: Grounded Correspondence with Aeronautical Ramifications

While settling and nurturing ways of behaving fundamentally happen on the ground, the correspondence related with territoriality has suggestions for ethereal elements. Birds use calls to lay out and protect regions, and these vocalizations add to the more extensive language of flight. Examining the exchange among territoriality and flight, this part investigates how grounded discussions resound into the skies, forming the flying scene.

IV. Past Flight Tunes: The Songs of Avian Correspondence
A. Inside and out Investigation of Bird Melodies
Bird tunes, with their melodic wealth and variety, structure a foundation of avian
correspondence. This part directs a top to bottom investigation of bird tunes,
disentangling the complexities of their design, capability, and versatile importance. From
the sunrise chorale to the songs of nighttime vocalists, the language of flight reaches
out to the domain of melodic correspondence, offering an orchestra that reverberates
across living spaces.

B. Tunes and Conceptive Ways of behaving
The captivating tunes of bird melodies fill needs past stylish charm. This part
investigates the association among tunes and regenerative ways of behaving, exploring
how avian vocalizations assume a significant part in romance ceremonies, mate
fascination, and the foundation of pair bonds. The language of flight turns into a heartfelt
poem, with every species forming its extraordinary stanzas to pass on messages of
adoration and conceptive wellness.

C. Provincial Varieties in Birdsong
As the language of flight traverses landmasses, local varieties in birdsong add a rich
layer to our investigation. From lingos inside an animal varieties to unmistakable
vocalizations remarkable to specific locales, the geological subtleties of bird
correspondence become obvious. This part leaves on a worldwide excursion, revealing
the social and territorial varieties that add to the different dictionary of avian
correspondence.

V. Dangers to the Language of Flight: Human Effects and Preservation Difficulties
A. Anthropogenic Clamor Contamination
The language of flight faces an impressive test as anthropogenic clamor contamination.
Human exercises present a bedlam of sounds that upset the acoustic scene birds
depend upon for correspondence. This segment investigates the effect of clamor
contamination on ethereal correspondence, from adjusted flight examples to
compromised conceptive achievement, and addresses potential protection procedures
to alleviate these impacts.

B. Territory Misfortune and Fracture
As normal territories lessen, the language of flight experiences the boundaries of natural
surroundings misfortune and discontinuity. The interruption of interconnected scenes
presents difficulties for transient birds, settling ways of behaving, and regional
correspondence.

Examining the repercussions of living space modification, this section stresses the significance of protection endeavors to safeguard the different discoursed that unfurl in the skies.

C. Environmental Change and Adjusted Relocation Examples

The changing environment presents another section in the language of flight, with adjusted relocation examples and changes in avian ways of behaving. This segment investigates the effect of environmental change on the fleeting and spatial elements of avian correspondence. Understanding these progressions becomes significant for protection drives pointed toward safeguarding the customary exchanges that have molded the skies for ages.

VI. Mechanical Advances: Snoopping on Airborne Discussions
A. Bioacoustics and Avian Correspondence Studies

Mechanical progressions in bioacoustics have changed the investigation of avian correspondence. This segment gives an outline of the devices and strategies that permit scientists to listen in on aeronautical discussions. From directional mouthpieces to computerized sound acknowledgment programming, bioacoustics turns into a strong focal point through which we gain remarkable bits of knowledge into the language of flight.

B. Following Innovations and Elevated Developments

Progressions in following advancements offer a brief look into the powerful developments of birds in flight. GPS beacons and satellite telemetry become significant instruments for understanding movement courses, searching examples, and the spatial elements of airborne correspondence. This part dives into the mechanical wonders that empower specialists to follow the excursions of birds across the skies.

C. Experiences Acquired and Future Prospects

The bits of knowledge acquired from mechanical developments shape the eventual fate of avian correspondence studies. From disentangling the importance behind complex flight examples to following the reactions of birds to natural changes, innovation opens new outskirts. This part investigates the significant commitments of these devices and imagines future opportunities for figuring out the developing language of flight.

1.1   Exploration of Aerial Communication

The domain of flying correspondence, where birds explore the skies with elegance and accuracy, is a spellbinding outskirts in the investigation of avian way of behaving. This investigation dives into the many-sided universe of avian talk in flight, unwinding the mysteries of correspondence that unfurl in the midst of the mists.

From the hypnotizing movement of relocation to the powerful discoursed of romance in mid-air, the skies become a material whereupon birds paint their accounts in the language of flight.

I. The Tastefulness of Movement: Elevated Movement Across Landmasses
Verifiable Points of view on Bird Movement

The peculiarity of bird relocation has interested humankind for a really long time. From old perceptions of occasional developments to current logical bits of knowledge, this part follows the verifiable points of view that have molded how we might interpret avian movement. Early naturalists wondered about the legendary excursions of birds, laying the basis for the acknowledgment of movement as an intricate and versatile way of behaving.

Exploring Immense Distances: Systems of Movement

The excursion into aeronautical correspondence starts with an investigation of how birds explore huge distances during relocation. Divine signs, attractive fields, and ecological elements unite to direct birds across mainlands. Examining these instruments gives experiences into the versatile meaning of movement, from getting to occasional assets to staying away from unfriendly climatic circumstances.

The Shared Language of Relocation: Rushing and Development Flying

As birds set out on their transitory excursions, the language of flight takes on a public aspect. Running way of behaving and development flying become vital to the account of avian correspondence. This part takes apart the complexities of these airborne presentations, featuring how birds speak with each other to upgrade effectiveness, decrease energy consumption, and explore the difficulties of significant distance flight.

II. Flying Discussions: The Elements of Mid-Air Correspondence
Romance Presentations overhead

The language of flight stretches out past down to earth contemplations to incorporate the domain of romance presentations. Birds take part in hypnotizing airborne exhibitions to draw in mates and lay out pair bonds. This segment divulges the gymnastic presentations of raptors, the synchronized trips of waterfowl, and the powerful exchanges that assume an essential part in mate choice and regenerative achievement.

Melodies and Brings in Flight: The Acoustic Scene of the Skies

As birds lift off, their correspondence collection grows to incorporate tunes and calls. Researching the acoustic scene of the skies uncovers how vocalizations fill needs going from an area protection to keeping in touch inside runs.

This segment investigates the transaction among visual and acoustic signs, featuring the unique idea of avian correspondence in flight.

III. Grounded Discussions: Settling, Nurturing, and Territoriality
Settling Ways of behaving: The Introduction to Flight
Prior to taking off, birds participate in grounded discussions related with settling ways of behaving. This part investigates the language of home development, mate choice, and the complexities of parental correspondence. From intricate romance ceremonies to agreeable endeavors in building homes, grounded exchanges set up for the airborne exhibitions that follow.

Parental Correspondence and Nestling Connection
When airborne, the language of flight stretches out to the domain of parental consideration. Parental correspondence includes a collection of vocalizations and motions pointed toward guaranteeing the prosperity of posterity. This part investigates the manners by which guardians speak with little birds, from food provisioning to showing fundamental abilities. The flying viewpoints offer an interesting vantage point for understanding the nuanced communications among guardians and their young.

Regional Calls: Grounded Correspondence with Flying Ramifications
While settling and nurturing ways of behaving fundamentally happen on the ground, the correspondence related with territoriality has suggestions for ethereal elements. Birds use calls to lay out and guard domains, and these vocalizations add to the more extensive language of flight. Examining the interchange among territoriality and flight, this segment investigates how grounded discussions resound into the skies, forming the elevated scene.

IV. Past Flight Tunes: The Songs of Avian Correspondence
Top to bottom Examination of Bird Tunes
Bird tunes, with their melodic extravagance and variety, structure a foundation of avian correspondence. This segment leads an inside and out examination of bird melodies, unwinding the complexities of their design, capability, and versatile importance. From the day break ensemble to the melodies of nighttime vocalists, the language of flight stretches out to the domain of melodic correspondence, offering an orchestra that reverberates across natural surroundings.
Tunes and Conceptive Ways of behaving
The captivating tunes of bird melodies fill needs past stylish appeal. This part investigates the association among tunes and conceptive ways of behaving, exploring how avian vocalizations assume a vital part in romance customs, mate fascination, and the foundation of pair bonds.

The language of flight turns into a heartfelt work, with every species making its interesting stanzas to pass on messages of affection and regenerative wellness.

Provincial Varieties in Birdsong
As the language of flight traverses mainlands, local varieties in birdsong add a rich layer to our investigation. From lingos inside an animal varieties to unmistakable vocalizations extraordinary to specific locales, this part sets out on a worldwide excursion, revealing the social and territorial varieties that add to the different vocabulary of avian correspondence.

V. Dangers to the Language of Flight: Human Effects and Protection Difficulties
Anthropogenic Commotion Contamination
The language of flight faces a considerable test as anthropogenic commotion contamination. Human exercises present a whirlwind of sounds that upset the acoustic scene birds depend upon for correspondence. This part investigates the effect of commotion contamination on flying correspondence, from changed flight examples to compromised conceptive achievement, and addresses potential preservation procedures to alleviate these impacts.

Living space Misfortune and Discontinuity
As regular environments reduce, the language of flight experiences the hindrances of territory misfortune and fracture. The disturbance of interconnected scenes presents difficulties for transient birds, settling ways of behaving, and regional correspondence. Exploring the repercussions of environment adjustment, this part underscores the significance of protection endeavors to safeguard the assorted discoursed that unfurl in the skies.

Environmental Change and Modified Relocation Examples
The changing environment presents another section in the language of flight, with adjusted relocation examples and changes in avian ways of behaving. This part investigates the effect of environmental change on the worldly and spatial elements of avian correspondence. Understanding these progressions becomes pivotal for preservation drives pointed toward safeguarding the customary discoursed that have molded the skies for ages.

VI. Innovative Advances: Snoopping on Elevated Discussions
Bioacoustics and Avian Correspondence Studies
Mechanical progressions in bioacoustics have changed the investigation of avian correspondence. This segment gives an outline of the apparatuses and strategies that permit scientists to listen in on airborne discussions.

From directional mouthpieces to robotized sound acknowledgment programming, bioacoustics turns into a strong focal point through which we gain remarkable experiences into the language of flight.

Following Innovations and Flying Developments
Progressions in following innovations offer a brief look into the powerful developments of birds in flight. GPS beacons and satellite telemetry become priceless apparatuses for understanding movement courses, scavenging designs, and the spatial elements of flying correspondence. This part dives into the mechanical wonders that empower specialists to follow the excursions of birds across the skies.

Experiences Acquired and Future Prospects
The bits of knowledge acquired from mechanical developments shape the fate of avian correspondence studies. From unraveling the importance behind complex flight examples to following the reactions of birds to ecological changes, innovation opens new outskirts. This part investigates the significant commitments of these apparatuses and imagines future opportunities for figuring out the developing language of flight.

1.2   Bird Migration Patterns and Communication Strategies

Bird relocation is a wonder of the regular world, a demonstration of the versatility and genius of avian species. This investigation digs into the many-sided examples of bird movement and the modern correspondence procedures that support these surprising excursions. From significant distance trips across landmasses to the nuanced exchanges that guide runs, bird relocation is a dynamic and complex peculiarity that mirrors the interconnectedness of avian life.

I. The Elements of Bird Movement
A. Authentic Points of view on Bird Movement
The peculiarity of bird relocation has spellbound human interest for quite a long time. Early naturalists wondered about the occasional developments of birds, with perceptions tracing all the way back to old times. This part gives a verifiable outline, featuring the movement of human comprehension from early stories to current logical experiences.

B. The Versatile Meaning of Relocation
Relocation isn't simply a conduct peculiarity; it is a method for surviving sharpened north of millions of years. This part investigates the versatile meaning of relocation, digging into the transformative tensions that have formed this peculiarity. From getting to occasional assets to staying away from unforgiving environments, the advantages of movement are necessary to the endurance and regenerative outcome of avian species.

C. Exploring Huge Distances: Components of Relocation

Birds undertaking transitory excursions face the overwhelming assignment of exploring immense distances with accuracy. This segment examines the components behind relocation, including divine signals, attractive fields, and ecological variables. Understanding how birds explore across landmasses gives experiences into the exceptional accomplishments of perseverance and route that portray transient excursions.

II. Correspondence Methodologies in Movement
A. Coordination inside Rushes: Running Way of behaving

Transient birds frequently travel in herds, and the coordination inside these gatherings is a demonstration of the viability of avian correspondence. Rushing conduct includes synchronized developments that improve effectiveness and diminish energy consumption. This segment investigates how birds convey inside runs during relocation, featuring the job of visual signs and the multifaceted movement that unfurls in the skies.

B. Vocalizations in Flight: Elevated Correspondence

While in flight, birds participate in airborne correspondence through vocalizations. These vocalizations fill different needs, from keeping in touch inside the group to flagging course adjustments. Exploring the acoustic scene of transitory excursions discloses the powerful exchanges that happen mid-air, adding to the general outcome of the movement.

C. Authority and Independent direction

Inside transitory herds, administration assumes a critical part in navigation. Certain people accept administrative roles, directing the herd in route and settling on basic choices. This part investigates the correspondence methodologies utilized in positions of authority, revealing insight into how compelling correspondence inside the herd adds to the general outcome of the relocation.

III. The Difficulties of Movement
A. Natural Perils and Transformations

Relocation isn't without difficulties, and birds experience different natural dangers during their excursions. From erratic weather conditions to geological impediments, transient species have advanced explicit variations to conquer these difficulties. This segment investigates the unpredictable interaction between ecological variables, correspondence procedures, and versatile ways of behaving.

B. Anthropogenic Effects

Human exercises acquaint extra difficulties with bird relocation. Anthropogenic elements, like urbanization, natural surroundings misfortune, and environmental change, upset customary transient courses and present new snags. Examining the effect of human exercises on transient examples features the significance of preservation endeavors to moderate these difficulties and safeguard the respectability of avian relocation.

IV. Innovative Experiences into Movement
A. Following Innovations and Exploration Advances

Mechanical developments have upset the investigation of bird relocation. Following innovations, including satellite telemetry and GPS gadgets, permit analysts to follow the courses of transient birds with remarkable accuracy. This segment investigates how these innovative advances give important experiences into relocation designs, visit areas, and the general elements of avian development.

B. Bioacoustics and Correspondence Exploration

Bioacoustics, the investigation of creature sounds, has turned into an integral asset for figuring out avian correspondence during movement. High level recording gadgets and mechanized sound acknowledgment programming empower scientists to dissect the vocalizations of birds in flight. This part dives into how bioacoustics adds to how we might interpret the correspondence methodologies utilized by transitory birds.

V. Protection Suggestions
A. Protecting Movement Hallways

Understanding bird relocation examples and correspondence procedures has direct ramifications for preservation. Saving movement hallways, the courses birds use during relocation, becomes fundamental for keeping up with the trustworthiness of these excursions. This segment accentuates the significance of preservation drives that consider the particular necessities of transitory species and the natural surroundings they depend upon.

B. Relieving Anthropogenic Dangers

Monitoring transient bird populaces requires tending to anthropogenic dangers. From limiting natural surroundings obliteration to alleviating environmental change influences, this part investigates the job of protection endeavors in defending transient courses. By understanding the difficulties birds face during movement, protection procedures can be custom-made to address explicit dangers.

VI. Contextual analyses: Unprecedented Transitory Excursions
A. The Icy Tern: Post to Shaft Ability

The Icy Tern brags one the most surprising transitory excursions, covering good ways from the Icy to the Antarctic and back. This contextual analysis digs into the correspondence techniques utilized by Icy Terns during their exceptional movement, revealing insight into the difficulties they face and the transformations that empower such really long travel.

B. The Ruler Butterfly: Airborne Trailblazers

While not birds, the transitory examples of the Ruler butterfly offer bits of knowledge into the more extensive topic of movement. This contextual investigation investigates the correspondence procedures utilized by Rulers during their mind boggling ventures and the preservation challenges they experience.

1.3   Interactions during Flight and their Significance

Flying isn't simply a method for transportation for birds; a dynamic and diverse action includes a heap of cooperations. Whether participated in synchronized flights, romance showcases, or regional questions, birds convey and communicate with momentous accuracy while in flight. This investigation digs into the different cooperations that happen during flight and looks at their importance with regards to avian way of behaving, correspondence, and endurance.

I. Synchronized Flights: The Expressive dance of Aggregate Development
A. Rushing Conduct

Quite possibly of the most spectacular exhibition in the avian world is the synchronized trip of a herd. Whether moving across huge distances or exploring neighborhood scenes, birds take part in rushing conduct that goes past simple coordination. This segment investigates the complexities of synchronized flights, where people move as a strong unit, exhibiting a degree of collaboration and correspondence that guarantees the productivity and security of the whole run.

B. Correspondence Inside Rushes

The synchronized developments inside a group are not erratic; they are a consequence of exact correspondence. Birds speak with one another during flight utilizing viewable signals, like course adjustments, speed, and arrangement. The importance lies in the aggregate dynamic cycle that permits the herd to answer natural improvements, dodge hunters, and explore complex territories.

II. Romance Showcases: Elevated Sentiment
A. Aerobatic Showcases

The skies become a phase for romance showcases as birds participate in stunning flying gymnastics to draw in mates. Raptors, waterfowl, and larks the same feature their spryness, strength, and plumage in mid-air exhibitions. This segment digs into the meaning of these romance presentations, investigating how they impart conceptive wellness, hereditary quality, and the readiness to put resources into the mating system.

B. Vocalizations and Tune in Flight

Romance reaches out past visual presentations to incorporate vocalizations and tune. Birds convey their goals and lay out bonds through melodic songs in flight. The importance lies in the job these flying melodies play in mate determination, match holding, and the foundation of regions, adding to the general outcome of the conceptive cycle.

III. Regional Connections: Protecting Airspace
A. Ethereal Domains

For the vast majority bird species, the idea of territoriality stretches out into the airspace. Birds vivaciously guard their aeronautical domains, participating in high-stakes communications to safeguard favorable places, rummaging regions, or settling locales. This part investigates the meaning of regional cooperations in flight, where correspondence through vocalizations, showcases, and aeronautical pursuits lays out and keeps up with limits.

B. Difficulties and Goals

Regional debates in the air can be extraordinary, including pursue groupings, plunges, and conflicts. The meaning of these communications lies in their job in settling clashes without turning to actual battle. Through correspondence and showcases of strength or accommodation, birds explore the intricate social elements of shared airspace, guaranteeing the productive utilization of assets and limiting the gamble of injury.

IV. Parental Consideration: Airborne Support
A. Taking care of in Flight

Parental consideration stretches out into the domain of trip as grown-up birds participate in taking care of ways of behaving while airborne. This segment looks at the meaning of taking care of associations in flight, where grown-ups give food to little birds or juveniles. The capacity to arrange taking care of developments in the air is vital for the endurance and advancement of the youthful, exhibiting the versatility of avian parental consideration systems.

B. Flying Correspondence with Little birds

Indeed, even in flight, guardians keep up with correspondence with their posterity. Vocalizations and explicit ways of behaving signal the presence of food, show fundamental abilities, and guarantee the prosperity of the little birds. This segment investigates how these elevated correspondence techniques add to the effective raising of the future and supports the parent-posterity bond.

V. Importance in Species Endurance
A. Transformative Benefits

The different associations during flight are not detached occasions yet rather developmental transformations that present benefits to bird species. Synchronized flights improve endurance during movement, romance presentations guarantee fruitful proliferation, regional associations keep up with asset access, and parental consideration in flight encourages the advancement of the future. Understanding the meaning of these communications gives experiences into the versatile systems that have permitted birds to flourish in assorted conditions.

B. Environmental Effect

The cooperations during flight have a more extensive environmental effect past individual species. Rushing ways of behaving add to biological system wellbeing by impacting prey-hunter elements, romance showcases add to hereditary variety and species lavishness, regional collaborations shape environment use, and parental consideration procedures impact populace elements. Perceiving the natural meaning of elevated associations highlights the interconnectedness of bird conduct and the strength of environments.

VI. Human Perceptions and Protection Suggestions
A. A Wellspring of Wonderment and Motivation

The associations saw during bird flight have interested people for quite a long time. From antiquated societies to advanced birdwatchers, the scene of synchronized flights, romance showcases, and regional communications has roused craftsmanship, writing, and logical request. This segment investigates the social and tasteful meaning of bird associations in flight, featuring the association between human appreciation and protection endeavors.

B. Preservation Difficulties and Arrangements

While the flying connections of birds spellbind human onlookers, they likewise face various difficulties in the anthropogenic world. Living space misfortune, environmental change, and human aggravations disturb the normal ways of behaving of birds in flight.

This segment examines the preservation ramifications of these difficulties and underscores the significance of protecting environments, limiting aggravations, and carrying out preservation techniques that consider the particular requirements of bird species participated in different airborne communications.

VII. Future Exploration and Unanswered Inquiries
A. Investigating the Boondocks

As how we might interpret bird cooperations during flight develops, new inquiries and boondocks arise. This segment investigates the potential for future examination, including the utilization of cutting edge innovations, for example, bioacoustics, radar, and telemetry to unwind the subtleties of ethereal correspondence. By diving into these neglected domains, analysts can develop how we might interpret the meaning of bird connections in flight and their job in the more extensive natural setting.

Chapter 2:
Grounded Conversations

In the period of fast mechanical progression, where correspondence is frequently decreased to instant messages, emoticons, and brief online entertainment refreshes, the idea of grounded discussions stands apart as a signal of significant collaboration. Grounded discussions, established in validness, profundity, and veritable association, offer an offset to the speedy, frequently shallow trades that rule our computerized scene. This investigation dives into the quintessence of grounded discussions, their importance in private and expert circles, and systems for cultivating them in a world driven by innovation.

I. Grasping Grounded Discussions
1. Characterizing Grounded Discussions
Grounded discussions can be portrayed by their profundity, earnestness, and the common trade of thoughts between people. Dissimilar to brief trades that occur in the computerized domain, grounded discussions rise above the surface, permitting members to investigate considerations, feelings, and encounters in a more significant way. They include undivided attention, sympathy, and a receptiveness to weakness.

2. The Significance of Validness
At the center of grounded discussions lies validness. Members carry their actual selves to the discourse, sharing their considerations, sentiments, and viewpoints without the apprehension about judgment. Legitimacy cultivates trust and establishes a climate where people can communicate their thoughts transparently, prompting more extravagant, additional satisfying collaborations.

II. The Computerized Challenge
1. The Effect of Innovation on Correspondence
The ascent of computerized correspondence stages has reformed the manner in which we associate with others. Notwithstanding, this comfort includes some significant downfalls. The curtness of instant messages, the restrictions of virtual entertainment, and the commonness of moment delight have added to a correspondence scene that frequently needs profundity. Grounded discussions, conversely, face difficulties in a world that values speed and proficiency over profundity and credibility.

2. Exploring Advanced Triviality

Tending to the difficulties presented by computerized correspondence requires a cognizant work to focus on grounded discussions. Systems like careful correspondence, saving devoted time for significant conversations, and embracing advanced instruments that work with profundity can assist people with exploring the traps of shallow internet based cooperation.

III. The Individual Domain: Grounded Discussions in Connections
1. Developing Associations

Grounded discussions assume a urgent part in encouraging significant connections, be they heartfelt, familial, or dispassionate. Investigating the elements of how profound, real correspondence adds to building and supporting associations gives bits of knowledge into the close to home parts of grounded discussions.

2. Supporting Ability to understand anyone on a deeper level

Grounded discussions add to the advancement of the capacity to appreciate people on a deeper level, upgrading one's capacity to comprehend and explore feelings, both one's own and those of others. This part digs into what the capacity to understand individuals on a deeper level sustained through grounded discussions can emphatically mean for individual connections and add to self-improvement.

IV. The Expert Circle: Grounded Discussions in the Work environment
1. Compelling Correspondence in Groups

Grounded discussions are urgent in the work environment, impacting cooperation, development, and representative fulfillment. This part investigates the job of grounded discussions in working with powerful correspondence inside groups, tending to clashes, and encouraging a positive work culture.

2. Authority and Grounded Discussions

Authority, when grounded in genuine correspondence, can groundbreakingly affect authoritative elements. Breaking down contextual analyses and best practices, this part looks at how pioneers who focus on grounded discussions add to representative commitment, hierarchical versatility, and development.

V. Procedures for Cultivating Grounded Discussions
1. Developing Undivided attention Abilities

Undivided attention is a foundation of grounded discussions. This segment gives functional tips and activities to improving undivided attention abilities, making an establishment for additional significant and significant connections.

2. Embracing Weakness

Weakness is much of the time seen as a shortcoming, however with regards to grounded discussions, it is a strength. This fragment investigates the idea of weakness and offers direction on how people can embrace and communicate weakness to develop associations.

3. Using Innovation Carefully

While innovation can be an obstruction to grounded discussions, it can likewise be a facilitator. This segment looks at how people can use innovation carefully to upgrade, instead of prevent, real correspondence.

VI. Conquering Boundaries to Grounded Discussions
1. Tending to Dread of Judgment

The anxiety toward judgment can hinder transparent correspondence. This portion investigates techniques for defeating this trepidation, establishing a climate where people have a solid sense of security to put themselves out there without reservation.

2. Using time effectively and Prioritization

In a high speed world, carving out opportunity for grounded discussions can be a test. This segment gives experiences into powerful using time effectively and prioritization methodologies, permitting people to assign time for significant connections in the midst of their bustling timetables.

2.1   Examination of Terrestrial Vocalizations

Earthbound vocalizations, the different cluster of sounds produced by animals occupying our planet, have long enamored the interest of researchers, naturalists, and devotees the same. From the frightful calls of whales reverberating through the sea profundities to the perplexing tunes of warblers in rich woods, Earth's animals impart through a complicated woven artwork of sounds. This assessment dives into the captivating universe of earthbound vocalizations, investigating their transformative importance, correspondence instruments, and the endeavors to decipher the intricate dialects that exist among natural creatures.

Transformative Meaning of Earthly Vocalizations:

The development of vocalizations in earthly living beings is well established in the methods for surviving of species across assorted biological systems. Vocalizations fill a huge number of needs, going from laying an out area and drawing in mates to advance notice of looming risk and organizing bunch exercises. The starting points of these sounds can be followed back great many years, addressing a versatile reaction to the difficulties introduced by the climate.

In the amphibian domain, marine well evolved creatures, for example, whales and dolphins have created unpredictable vocal collections for correspondence in the huge fields of the sea. Whale tunes, for example, are accepted to assume a significant part in significant distance correspondence and mate fascination. These complicated vocalizations are a demonstration of the social designs and insight of these glorious animals.

Ashore, birds have advanced an unprecedented variety of vocalizations, going from sweet melodies to multifaceted calls. Birdsong isn't only a result of avian presence however a crucial part of their way of behaving, impacting mate choice, regional protection, and route. The mimicry capacities of specific bird species, like the lyrebird and the great lyrebird, feature the association among vocalizations and conceptive achievement.

Correspondence Components in Earthly Vocalizations:

The investigation of earthly vocalizations includes disentangling the unpredictable snare of correspondence instruments utilized by various species. While certain creatures utilize straightforward calls to pass on fundamental data, others participate in intricate vocal exhibitions that require a profound comprehension of their social elements.

One remarkable model is the bumble bee, known for its mind boggling waggle dance, a type of correspondence that passes the area of food sources on to different individuals from the hive. Through exact developments and vibrations, a searching honey bee can impart the distance, heading, and nature of a food source, empowering proficient asset double-dealing by the state.

In the primate world, including species like chimpanzees and bonobos, vocalizations assume a urgent part in communicating feelings, laying out friendly orders, and planning bunch exercises. These vocal signs, frequently joined by motions and looks, structure a refined arrangement of correspondence that adds to the union of primate social orders.

Translating the Language of Natural Creatures:

Endeavors to translate earthly vocalizations have strengthened with progressions in innovation and a developing appreciation for the intricacy of creature correspondence. Bioacoustics, a multidisciplinary field that consolidates science, acoustics, and software engineering, has arisen as a vital device in this undertaking.

One of the most celebrated examples of overcoming adversity in the field of bioacoustics is the investigation of cetacean correspondence. Scientists have utilized hydrophones and submerged recording gadgets to catch and dissect the unpredictable vocalizations of whales and dolphins.

Through broad investigations, unmistakable examples and tongues inside these species have been distinguished, revealing insight into their social designs and transitory ways of behaving.

In the avian domain, the advancement of modern recording hardware and computational examination devices has empowered scientists to dig into the intricacy of bird tunes. The tunes of specific species, like the songbird and the canary, are tastefully satisfying as well as act as a rich wellspring of data about the wellbeing and hereditary wellness of individual birds.

Headways in man-made reasoning and AI have additionally sped up the examination of earthbound vocalizations. These innovations permit specialists to handle tremendous measures of sound information, recognize examples, and even recognize individual voices inside a populace. Subsequently, the complex subtleties of correspondence inside species are being revealed, giving significant bits of knowledge into their way of behaving and environment.

Challenges and Moral Contemplations:
While the investigation of earthbound vocalizations has yielded momentous disclosures, it isn't without its difficulties and moral contemplations. One unmistakable test is the immense variety of vocalizations across species, making it a complicated undertaking to foster widespread systems for investigation. Moreover, the fluctuation in ecological circumstances and the impact of human exercises on normal territories present difficulties in precisely deciphering creature sounds.

Moral contemplations become possibly the most important factor, especially in examinations including the playback of recorded vocalizations to creatures. The potential for disturbing normal ways of behaving, causing pressure, or modifying the elements of creature populaces brings up moral issues about the effect of exploration exercises on the concentrated on organic entities. Finding some kind of harmony between logical request and moral obligation is urgent in guaranteeing the prosperity of the subjects in question.

Protection Suggestions:
Understanding earthbound vocalizations isn't just a logical pursuit yet additionally holds significant ramifications for protection endeavors. The vocalizations of numerous species act as marks of biological system wellbeing, giving early admonitions of ecological changes and aggravations.

For example, changes in the vocal way of behaving of creatures of land and water, frequently alluded to as "acoustic biology," have been connected to natural stressors like contamination and territory debasement.

Checking these vocalizations can offer experiences into the effect of human exercises on land and water proficient populaces and guide protection systems to alleviate these dangers.

Likewise, the investigation of bird vocalizations can add to the protection of avian biodiversity. Distinguishing key vocalization examples can help with checking populace patterns, surveying the outcome of rearing projects, and recognizing basic territories for assurance.

2.2   Calls for Territory Establishment and Defense

In the immense and perplexing embroidery of the normal world, the calls produced by creatures for region foundation and guard act as an ensemble of endurance. These vocalizations, various and deliberate, assume a significant part in forming the social elements and environmental cooperations of species across various biological systems. This investigation digs into the entrancing domain of regional calls, looking at their developmental importance, the systems hidden their demeanor, and the complex dance of correspondence that unfurls inside the animals of the world collectively.

Developmental Meaning of Regional Calls:

Territoriality, the protection and foundation of a characterized space, is a far reaching peculiarity in the set of all animals, driven by the need to get assets, guarantee conceptive achievement, and lay out friendly orders. Regional calls have developed as a urgent part of this versatile way of behaving, addressing a refined method for correspondence that assists people with exploring the intricate elements of sharing and shielding space.

In the avian world, regional calls are noticeably shown through the melodic tunes of warblers. These tunes not just act as hear-able reference points to lay out and protect domains yet in addition assume an essential part in drawing in mates. The advancement of intricate tunes in birds mirrors the significance of viable correspondence in getting regenerative achievement and keeping up with regional limits.

Warm blooded creatures, as well, display a rich cluster of regional calls. The notable thunder of a lion reverberating across the savannah or the ghostly wails of wolves in thick backwoods are instances of vocalizations used to delineate and guard regions. These calls serve as admonitions to possible interlopers as well as statements of strength inside a gathering.

Components of Regional Calls:
The instruments hidden regional calls are assorted, mirroring the novel transformations of various species to their surroundings and social designs. From synthetic motioning toward complex vocalizations, creatures utilize various strategies to impart their regional presence and goals.
In the bug world, pheromones assume an essential part in stamping and shielding domains. Subterranean insects, for instance, discharge pheromones to lay out trails prompting food sources and to separate the limits of their states. These synthetic signs act as a compelling method for correspondence, permitting insects to arrange exercises and shield their region against rival states.

Interestingly, the avian domain depends vigorously on vocalizations for regional correspondence. Birds utilize a blend of calls and tunes, each filling a particular need. While calls might convey prompt dangers or admonitions, tunes are many times intricate and melodic, working as both regional markers and signs of conceptive wellness. The complexity of bird tunes mirrors the specific tensions that have formed these vocalizations over ages.
Warm blooded creatures, particularly those with complex social designs, utilize a mix of vocalizations and actual presentations to lay out and protect regions. The low-recurrence thunders of enormous felines, for example, can go over significant distances, filling in as a powerful method for correspondence in open scenes. Conversely, primates might participate in a blend of vocalizations, for example, hooting or drumming, and actual presentations to declare strength and depict regional limits.

Connections and Correspondence Elements:
The foundation and protection of regions include complex correspondence elements inside and between species. Regional calls are signals for conspecifics as well as pass on data about the personality, status, and goals of the guest. Understanding these correspondence elements gives experiences into the intricacies of creature conduct and the systems utilized for endurance.
In many bird species, the sunrise tune addresses a common regional showcase, with people adding to the orchestra of calls that resound through the early morning air. This synchronized vocalization supports regional limits as well as conveys the wealth of vocal and actual assets inside the domain. The power and variety of the day break melody can be characteristic of the wellbeing and imperativeness of a specific living space.

Regional questions, a typical event in the set of all animals, frequently include extreme vocal trades and actual showdowns. At times, for example, the conflicts between rival male lions, thunders might grow into wild fights for strength and control of an area.

These collaborations, while apparently forceful, assume a significant part in keeping social control and forestalling superfluous struggles that could be unfavorable to the endurance of people inside a populace.

The Job of Ecological Elements:
Ecological elements assume a critical part in forming the articulation and viability of regional calls. Acoustic properties of the natural surroundings, like vegetation thickness, geography, and encompassing commotion levels, can impact the transmission and gathering of vocal signs. Understanding how creatures adjust their correspondence systems to various conditions gives important experiences into the biological elements of domains.
In thick woods, where obvious signs might be restricted, birds frequently depend on perplexing vocalizations to lay out and protect regions. The mind boggling construction of the woods shelter can impact the transmission of sound, prompting the advancement of remarkable calls that are appropriate to the acoustic difficulties of these conditions. Likewise, in open scenes, where perceivability is high, visual showcases might supplement vocalizations in the foundation and safeguard of regions.

Anthropogenic variables, like urbanization and environment discontinuity, represent extra difficulties to the correspondence elements of regional calls. Expanded clamor contamination, for instance, can slow down the transmission of vocal signs, upsetting the capacity of creatures to really convey inside and between regions. Protection endeavors pointed toward moderating these effects are vital for the conservation of regular correspondence frameworks and the natural respectability of living spaces.

Contextual analyses in Regional Correspondence:
Looking at explicit contextual analyses in regional correspondence gives a more profound comprehension of the variety and intricacy of these ways of behaving across various taxa.

Birdsong in Larks:
Larks, or passerines, are prestigious for their intricate tunes that assume a focal part in regional correspondence. Every species displays novel melody designs, frequently went down through ages. Concentrates on the incredible tit (Parus major), for instance, have uncovered that youthful guys become familiar with the melodies of more seasoned, more fruitful people, adding to the social transmission of regional signs inside a populace. The lavishness of bird tune reflects hereditary variables as well as the social trade of data inside a local area.

Crying in Wolves:
Wolves are known for their unpleasant yells, which act as regional markers and correspondence signals inside a pack. Research on wolf vocalizations has distinguished unmistakable yelling designs related with various settings, including region safeguard, pack coordination, and mate fascination. The orchestrated yells of a wolf pack make a strong acoustic showcase that supports social securities and discourages possible gatecrashers.

Elephant Thunders:
Elephants, with their exceptionally evolved social designs, use infrasound, or low-recurrence sounds underneath the scope of human hearing, for regional correspondence. Elephant thunders, delivered by vocal folds in the larynx, can go over significant distances and pass on data about the size and strength of a person. Studies have demonstrated the way that elephants can separate between the thunders of recognizable and new people, featuring the nuanced idea of their correspondence.

Protection Suggestions:
Understanding regional calls has significant ramifications for protection endeavors, especially notwithstanding continuous dangers, for example, living space misfortune, environmental change, and human-untamed life struggle. Territoriality, as an essential part of creature conduct, is firmly connected to the accessibility and nature of living spaces. Preservation methodologies that perceive and safeguard the biological meaning of regions are fundamental for guaranteeing the endurance of species and keeping up with biodiversity.

Territory Conservation:
Perceiving the significance of regions in the existence chronicles of species is basic to living space conservation. Preservation endeavors ought to focus on the security of key living spaces that act as basic regions for rearing, taking care of, and other fundamental exercises. Recognizing and defending these regions add to the general wellbeing and versatility of populaces.

Hall Protection:
Territoriality frequently includes development between various regions, and laying out environmental passageways that interface divided living spaces is essential for keeping up with hereditary variety and working with regular ways of behaving. Passageway preservation permits creatures to cross domains, access assets, and participate in fundamental exercises, adding to the drawn out suitability of populaces.

Relieving Human-Untamed life Struggle:
As human populaces grow and infringe upon normal living spaces, clashes among people and untamed life over domain can raise. Executing successful systems to relieve these contentions, for example, the improvement of feasible land-use rehearses and the utilization of non-deadly hindrances, is essential for conjunction. Understanding the correspondence elements of regional calls can illuminate the plan regarding mediations that limit negative communications.

Tending to Environmental Change Effects:
Environmental change represents a danger to biological systems around the world, influencing the accessibility of assets and modifying natural surroundings reasonableness. Regional species might confront provokes in adjusting to these changes, requiring proactive protection measures. Checking shifts in regional ways of behaving and changing protection techniques appropriately can assist with alleviating the effects of environmental change on weak populaces.

2.3   Parental Communication and Nesting Behaviors

Parental correspondence and settling ways of behaving are fundamental parts of everyday life in the set of all animals, addressing a perplexing exchange of impulses, variations, and social elements. Across different biological systems, species have advanced interesting techniques to guarantee the endurance and prosperity of their posterity. This investigation digs into the entrancing universe of parental correspondence and settling ways of behaving, analyzing their transformative importance, the assorted components utilized, and the basic job they play in molding the people in the future of different creatures.

Transformative Meaning of Parental Correspondence:
Parental correspondence is a foundation of conceptive achievement, working with coordination among mates and guaranteeing the legitimate consideration and insurance of posterity. All through transformative history, species have fostered a different cluster of correspondence systems to explore the difficulties of being a parent and upgrade the possibilities of their descendants arriving at development.

Mate Choice and Match Holding:
Correspondence between mates starts with the course of mate choice and match holding. Numerous species take part in intricate romance ceremonies including visual showcases, vocalizations, and compound signs. These romance ways of behaving effectively survey the hereditary wellness of possible mates, lay out similarity, and reinforce the connection between accomplices, establishing the groundwork for fruitful nurturing.

Coordination of Regenerative Exercises:

When matched, parental correspondence stretches out to the coordination of conceptive exercises. In birds, for instance, mate matches participate in synchronized showcases and vocalizations to flag status for lovemaking and egg-laying. The timing and accuracy of these signs are basic for the fruitful turn of events and bring forth of eggs, exhibiting the significance of compelling correspondence in the beginning phases of life as a parent.

Components of Parental Correspondence:

The components of parental correspondence are assorted, incorporating visual, hear-able, olfactory, and material signs. These signs fill various needs at different phases of the conceptive interaction, from mate choice to posterity care.

Visual Signs:

Visual signs are noticeable in numerous species during romance and the foundation of pair bonds. Energetic plumage, mind boggling showcases, and body developments add to the visual language of parental correspondence. Peacocks, for example, grandstand their striking plumage to draw in mates, while moving and showing ways of behaving act as viewable prompts in many bird species.

Hear-able Signs:

Hear-able correspondence assumes a urgent part in the coordination of regenerative exercises and the support of social bonds. Birds, creatures of land and water, and warm blooded animals frequently use vocalizations to pass on data about their regenerative status, caution of expected dangers, and direction parental obligations. The melodic tunes of larks and the musical croaking of frogs are instances of hear-able signs utilized in parental correspondence.

Olfactory and Compound Signs:

Olfactory and substance signals are especially significant in warm blooded animals and certain bug species. Warm blooded animals, including canids and felids, use aroma checking to lay out domains, impart regenerative status, and recognize people. In bugs like subterranean insects and honey bees, synthetic signs called pheromones assume a critical part in planning regenerative exercises and coordinating the social construction of settlements.

Settling Ways of behaving and Parental Consideration:

Settling ways of behaving are one more feature of parental venture, addressing the development and upkeep of a reasonable climate for the raising of posterity.

Settling ways of behaving shift generally across taxa and are adjusted to the natural specialty and life history of every species.

Home Development:
The development of homes is a general settling conduct saw in different life forms. Birds fabricate homes utilizing materials like twigs, leaves, and quills, making a solid and protected space for eggs and little birds. Warm blooded animals, for example, rodents, develop tunnels or homes from vegetation to give security to their young. The design variety of homes mirrors the versatile methodologies utilized by every species to meet the particular requirements of their posterity.

Egg Brooding:
Brooding of eggs is a basic settling conduct that guarantees the legitimate improvement of undeveloped organisms. Birds, specifically, show different brooding systems, with the two guardians sharing the obligation in certain species. Penguins, for instance, alternate hatching eggs on their feet, while gooney birds and hawks take part in extensive stretches of shared brooding obligations.

Parental Consideration and Provisioning:
Parental consideration reaches out past home development and brooding to incorporate the provisioning and security of posterity. Warm blooded creatures frequently medical caretaker and lucky man their young, giving fundamental supplements and guaranteeing cleanliness. In birds, guardians take part in searching exercises to take care of little birds, showing a momentous coordination of parental jobs to meet the wholesome necessities of their posterity.

Developmental Variations and Systems:
Parental correspondence and settling ways of behaving are molded by a horde of transformative variations that improve the possibilities of regenerative achievement. The variety of these techniques mirrors the particular tensions looked by species in their separate surroundings.

Altricial versus Precocial Posterity:
The degree of parental venture frequently relates with the formative phase of posterity upon entering the world or incubating. Species with altricial posterity, like most birds and a few vertebrates, put vigorously in parental consideration, giving sustenance, security, and warmth until the youthful are equipped for free endurance. Conversely, species with precocial posterity, like a few ungulates and precocial birds, put more in home development and depend on the youthful's capacity to move and scrounge not long after birth.

Parental Venture and Social Design:
The social design of an animal types impacts the conveyance of parental obligations. In monogamous species, the two guardians ordinarily add to settle building, brooding, and posterity care. Polygamous species, then again, may display varieties in parental venture, with one parent expecting a more prominent portion of providing care obligations.

Helpful Reproducing:
Helpful reproducing, saw in different bird species and a few well evolved creatures, includes extra people aiding the consideration of posterity. This agreeable exertion upgrades the endurance chances of the youthful and might be driven by family determination or biological variables that make collective nurturing profitable.

Preservation Suggestions:
Understanding the complexities of parental correspondence and settling ways of behaving is critical for informed preservation endeavors. As living spaces face expanding dangers, preservation techniques should consider the exceptional regenerative methodologies of various species to safeguard and save biodiversity actually.

Territory Safeguarding:
Protecting assorted territories is fundamental for the continuation of species-explicit settling ways of behaving. Settling destinations, whether tunnels, trees, or ground homes, should be defended to guarantee the accessibility of appropriate conditions for reproducing and raising posterity.

Relieving Anthropogenic Aggravations:
Human exercises, like deforestation and urbanization, can disturb settling ways of behaving and parental correspondence. Relieving these aggravations and executing supportable land-use rehearses are basic for limiting the effect on regenerative achievement and keeping up with solid populaces.

Preservation of Key Species:
Species with exceptional settling ways of behaving or those showing specific parental consideration techniques might be especially helpless against ecological changes. Preservation endeavors ought to focus on the assurance of these key species, perceiving their job in keeping up with environment elements.

Chapter 3:
Beyond Song: The Melodies of Nature

In the fabulous ensemble of life on The planet, nature coordinates an enthralling creation of sounds that rise above the limits of human music. Past the old songs of birdsong, the tunes of nature reverberate through woods, seas, and skies, winding around a mind boggling embroidery of correspondence, variation, and environmental concordance. This investigation digs into the assorted hints of the regular world, from the musical stir of passes on to the eerie calls of whales, uncovering the significant meaning of these tunes in understanding and valuing the interconnectedness of every living thing.

The Language of the Breeze:
The breeze, a delicate director in nature's symphony, murmurs through leaves, moans across huge scenes, and wails through gullies. The language of the breeze, communicated through the stirring of leaves, conveys fundamental data about the climate. Trees, furnished with a heap of shapes and surfaces, make special sounds when stroked by the breeze. The shuddering leaves of aspen trees, for instance, produce an unmistakable tremolo, while the solid needles of pine trees create a delicate susurrus. This orchestra of stirring passes on not just adds a lovely quality to the regular world yet additionally fills in as a type of correspondence.
In environments, the breeze assumes a vital part in the dispersal of seeds and dust. Certain plants, similar to dandelions, have developed structures that use the breeze to convey their seeds over significant distances, guaranteeing hereditary variety and the extension of their populaces. The songs of the breeze, consequently, add to the biological dance of propagation and endurance.

Sea-going Harmonies:
Underneath the outer layer of seas, waterways, and lakes, a different scope of sea-going songs unfurls. Marine life, from the littlest scavangers to the biggest whales, imparts through an ensemble of snaps, whistles, and melodies. Whales, specifically, are eminent for their unpredictable vocalizations, which fill different needs, including route, mate fascination, and social holding.

The frightful and complex tunes of humpback whales, for instance, can convey across huge distances submerged. These tunes, made out of rehashed examples and subjects, are remembered to assume a part in mating ceremonies and keeping up with social bonds inside whale populaces. The investigation of these marine tunes not just gives experiences into the way of behaving of these superb animals yet in addition features the significance of acoustic correspondence in the immense region of the sea. Underneath the waves, the melody of marine life stretches out to the hypnotizing hints of coral reefs. Coral reefs, frequently alluded to as the rainforests of the ocean, are overflowing with a different cluster of living beings that add to the energetic ensemble of submerged life. The popping of snapping shrimp, the pops of fish correspondence, and the delicate murmur of coral polyps on the whole structure a many-sided and amicable amphibian creation.

Avian Crescendos:
Birdsong, a generally perceived song of the regular world, holds a focal spot in the orchestra of nature. Past its tasteful allure, bird correspondence serves fundamental capabilities like mate fascination, region foundation, and cautioning of expected dangers. The tunes of birds are in many cases complex, for certain species fit for impersonating a large number of sounds, including the calls of other bird species and, surprisingly, human-made commotions.
The first light melody, an aggregate eruption of bird vocalizations that happens during the early hours of the day, is an especially charming peculiarity. It includes various bird species participating in a synchronized showcase of tunes, making a rich embroidery of sound that consumes the space. The sunrise tune isn't just a delightful regular scene yet additionally serves significant biological capabilities, for example, supporting regional limits and planning rearing exercises.

Notwithstanding vocalizations, birds utilize different non-vocal sounds for correspondence. Drumming, for instance, is a percussive sound created by woodpeckers striking their mouths against resounding surfaces like trees. This musical drumming fills in as a type of correspondence among people and can assume a part in drawing in mates or guarding regions.

Bug Cadenzas:
The universe of bugs is loaded up with a racket of sounds, from the delicate humming of honey bees to the cadenced trilling of crickets. Bugs impart through various instruments, including stridulation, the development of sound by scouring body parts together. This is outstandingly seen in crickets, grasshoppers, and katydids, where specific designs on their wings or legs produce unmistakable calls.

The buzz of honey bees, notwithstanding its job in correspondence inside the hive, is fundamental for fertilization. As honey bees move from one blossom to another, their humming vibrates dust, working with the exchange of regenerative material and guaranteeing the proceeded with development of plants. The tunes of bugs, frequently neglected or excused as foundation commotion, are unpredictably associated with the environmental working of biological systems.

Land and water proficient and Reptilian Songs:
Creatures of land and water, with their penetrable skin and amphibian rearing propensities, contribute special sounds to the orchestra of nature. Frogs and amphibians, specifically, are known for their vocalizations, which range from melodic calls to musical croaks. These calls are fundamental for mate fascination and laying out regions during the reproducing season.
The calls of creatures of land and water can shift fundamentally among species and are impacted by variables like ecological circumstances and individual variety. The soundscape made by creatures of land and water in wetlands and bogs isn't just a demonstration of the variety of life yet in addition fills in as a mark of environment wellbeing. The decrease in land and water proficient populaces and the modification of their vocalization examples can flag natural stressors and the requirement for preservation mediations.

Reptiles, albeit not normally connected with vocalizations, additionally add to the regular soundscape. A few reptiles, for example, snakes and reptiles, produce murmurs or clatters as an advance notice sign to possible hunters. Turtle species take part in different vocalizations, including murmurs, snorts, and trills, frequently as a type of correspondence during romance and mating.

Mammalian Murmurs:
Vertebrates, going from the littlest rodents to the biggest land-staying animals, convey through a rich exhibit of vocalizations and different sounds. Past the famous thunders of enormous felines and the trumpeting of elephants, well evolved creatures utilize various inconspicuous sounds for correspondence, route, and social holding.
Rodents, for instance, may create ultrasonic vocalizations that are past the scope of human hearing. These ultrasonic calls assume a part in correspondence between people, especially in friendly species. Bats, one more gathering of vertebrates, explore and find prey utilizing echolocation — a natural sonar framework including the outflow of high-recurrence calls and the translation of returning reverberations.

In the immense scenes of the Icy, the ethereal soundscape of ice and snow turns into a basic piece of the regular tune. The breaking and squeaking of icy masses, the far off calls of marine warm blooded creatures, and the delicate cushioning of Cold foxes on snow-shrouded landscape make a supernatural orchestra. These sounds not just add to the tactile experience of the Icy yet in addition assume a part in the step by step processes for surviving of its occupants.

Human Effect on Normal Tunes:
As human exercises keep on modifying scenes and living spaces, the regular tunes of the Earth face new difficulties. Urbanization, deforestation, and environmental change can upset the mind boggling equilibrium of normal soundscapes, influencing the correspondence, route, and step by step processes for surviving of innumerable species.

Commotion Contamination:
Perhaps of the main anthropogenic effect on regular songs is commotion contamination. Metropolitan conditions, described by consistent traffic, modern exercises, and human turn of events, make a chaos that can cover or upset the normal hints of biological systems. This impedance can adversely affect correspondence among species, possibly prompting changes in conduct, rearing examples, and hunter prey associations.

Natural surroundings Discontinuity:
Natural surroundings discontinuity, a result of human turn of events, can disengage populaces and disturb the interconnectedness of environments. This discontinuity can restrict the capacity of species to impart over enormous distances and hinder the regular progression of sounds through scenes. Preservation endeavors that focus on territory network are critical for keeping up with the respectability of normal soundscapes.

Environmental Change:
Environmental change, with its related effects on temperature, precipitation, and ocean levels, can adjust the acoustic properties of conditions. Changes in vegetation designs, the softening of ice, and changes in sea flows can all add to adjustments in regular soundscapes. Understanding the manners by which environmental change impacts the songs of nature is fundamental for anticipating and alleviating its consequences for biodiversity.

3.1   In-depth Analysis of Bird Songs

Bird melodies, with their melodic tunes and complex examples, have intrigued people for quite a long time. Past their tasteful allure, bird melodies assume a critical part in avian correspondence, mirroring the assorted ways of behaving, social designs, and biological transformations of various species. This top to bottom examination dives into the universe of bird melodies, investigating their transformative beginnings, the components basic their creation, the capabilities they serve in avian social orders, and the social importance they hold for the two people and birds.

Transformative Beginnings of Bird Melodies:

The development of bird tunes is a captivating excursion interwoven with the historical backdrop of avian species. While not all birds are larks, many have fostered the capacity to deliver complex vocalizations. The starting points of bird melodies can be followed back to the requirement for correspondence in different settings, including mate fascination, region protection, and coordination inside gatherings.

Mate Fascination and Regenerative Achievement:

One of the essential elements of bird melodies is mate fascination. Male birds frequently utilize elaborate melodies to flag their presence, hereditary wellness, and region quality to likely mates. The intricacy and power of these tunes can impact a female's decision of mate, straightforwardly influencing conceptive achievement. After some time, the capacity to create engaging melodies turned into a specific benefit, adding to the development of assorted and unpredictable vocalizations in various species.

Domain Protection and Correspondence:

Bird melodies are instrumental in laying out and protecting domains. Numerous species use vocalizations to separate limits, caution interlopers, and direction exercises inside gatherings. The foundation of domains directs admittance to assets, diminish rivalry, and guarantee the prosperity of people inside a populace. The development of regional melodies mirrors the versatile procedures utilized by birds to effectively explore their surroundings.

Components of Bird Tune Creation:

The development of bird tunes includes a blend of physical, physiological, and brain systems. Understanding these components gives experiences into the striking intricacy and variety of avian vocalizations.

Syrinx, the Avian Vocal Organ:

The syrinx, an interesting avian vocal organ situated at the foundation of the windpipe, is vital to the development of bird melodies.

Not at all like the vocal strings of warm blooded creatures, the syrinx permits birds to deliver many sounds and unpredictable tunes. Its construction comprises of muscles, layers, and ligament that can be controlled with noteworthy accuracy. The syrinx's adaptability and intricacy add to the variety of bird tunes across species.

Brain Control of Melody Creation:
The brain control of bird melody creation includes complex connections between the mind, sensory system, and muscles. In larks, a particular cerebrum district known as the tune control framework oversees the learning and creation of melodies. The educational experience includes openness to conspecific tunes during a basic period in early life, featuring the job of both hereditary inclination and natural impacts in forming individual melody collections.

Learning and Social Transmission:
Bird melodies, especially in warblers, are learned ways of behaving. Youthful birds procure their melodies by mirroring the vocalizations of grown-up conspecifics, frequently including components of social transmission inside populaces. Social varieties in tunes can arise, prompting particular territorial lingos and exceptional collections inside unambiguous networks. The capacity to learn and send melodies socially upgrades the adaptability and versatility of avian correspondence.

Elements of Bird Melodies in Avian Social orders:
Bird melodies serve a large number of capabilities inside avian social orders, adding to individual wellness, social elements, and conceptive achievement. The assorted jobs of bird melodies feature the versatility of these vocalizations across various environmental specialties.

Mate Fascination and Match Holding:
The essential capability of bird tunes in numerous species is mate fascination. Male birds utilize their tunes to publicize their presence, convey their hereditary wellness, and lay out regions that draw in likely mates. Fruitful romance frequently prompts the arrangement of pair bonds, with shared vocalizations adding to the upkeep of these bonds over the long run.

Region Foundation and Safeguard:
Bird melodies assume a critical part in characterizing and protecting domains. The vocalizations of guys act as regional markers, discouraging expected interlopers and flagging responsibility for regions. Intraspecific contentions over regions are much of the time settled through vocal trades, limiting actual showdowns and decreasing the gamble of injury.

Coordination inside Gatherings:

Inside friendly bird species, melodies work with correspondence and coordination inside gatherings. Vocalizations can pass on data about food sources, likely dangers, and the general prosperity of people inside a local area. Agreeable reproducing species, where numerous people add to raising posterity, depend on mind boggling vocal trades to synchronize exercises and guarantee the progress of the gathering.

Parent-Posterity Correspondence:

Parental consideration and correspondence with posterity are fundamental parts of avian life. Bird guardians utilize explicit vocalizations to speak with their chicks, passing on data about taking care of, wellbeing, and the area of the home. Chicks, thusly, answer with asking calls that invigorate parental provisioning, making a powerful correspondence framework among guardians and posterity.

Social Meaning of Bird Melodies:

The social meaning of bird melodies reaches out past the domain of avian correspondence, catching the human creative mind and impacting different parts of workmanship, writing, and custom.

Motivation for Human Craftsmanship and Music:

Bird melodies have been a wellspring of motivation for human specialists and performers from the beginning of time. The multifaceted tunes, musical examples, and different tones of bird vocalizations have tracked down their direction into creations, writing, and visual workmanship. From old style music to contemporary sorts, birdsong themes are woven into the texture of human inventiveness, inspiring an association between the regular world and imaginative articulation.

Imagery and Social Portrayals:

Birds and their melodies frequently hold representative importance in different societies. The songbird, commended for its strong and sweet melody, is a common image in writing and folklore, addressing adoration, magnificence, and the otherworldly force of music. Also, the eerie calls of owls and the magnificent tunes of raptors convey emblematic implications across various societies, molding impression of these birds in fables and customs.

Logical and Instructive Worth:

Bird tunes assume a crucial part in logical examination and training. Ornithologists and ethologists utilize the investigation of bird vocalizations to acquire experiences into avian way of behaving, environment, and developmental cycles.

Birdwatchers and lovers utilize the ID of melodies as a critical device in birding, improving comprehension they might interpret avian variety and adding to resident science drives zeroed in on observing bird populaces.

Preservation and Ecotourism:
The enthusiasm for bird melodies has direct ramifications for protection endeavors. Birds, frequently viewed as ecological pointers, signal the wellbeing of biological systems through their vocalizations. The appeal of birdwatching, powered by the craving to notice and distinguish bird species in view of their melodies, has added to the development of ecotourism and preservation mindfulness. The preservation of avian living spaces and the conservation of normal soundscapes become necessary parts of endeavors to safeguard biodiversity.

Progressing Exploration and Mechanical Advances:
Progressions in innovation have changed the investigation of bird melodies, permitting analysts to dig further into the complexities of avian correspondence.

Bioacoustics and Computerized Investigation:
Bioacoustics, the investigation of organic sounds, has turned into a useful asset in the examination of bird melodies. Mechanized recording gadgets, furnished with modern programming, empower specialists to gather enormous datasets of bird vocalizations in different conditions. This innovation works with the distinguishing proof of individual species, the measurement of vocal way of behaving, and the investigation of changes in bird populaces after some time.

Neuroethology and Brain Planning:
Neuroethological research centers around unwinding the brain systems hidden bird melody creation and learning. Progresses in brain planning methods have permitted researchers to follow the brain connections engaged with the creation and view of bird tunes. Understanding the neurobiology of bird tunes improves our appreciation of the complex cycles associated with avian correspondence and the development of vocal learning.

Resident Science and Publicly supported Information:
Resident science drives, powered by the commitment of birdwatchers and nature devotees, contribute significant information to the investigation of bird melodies. Portable applications and online stages permit people to record and share bird vocalizations, adding to enormous scope data sets utilized in logical examination.

Publicly supported information assume a significant part in checking bird populaces, following changes in vocal way of behaving, and recognizing arising designs in avian correspondence.

Preservation Suggestions:
The investigation of bird tunes has direct ramifications for avian protection and environment the executives.

Natural surroundings Protection:
The conservation of normal living spaces is fundamental for keeping up with the honesty of bird tunes and supporting avian biodiversity. Living space misfortune, fracture, and corruption can disturb avian correspondence, influencing mate fascination, region foundation, and in general conceptive achievement. Preservation endeavors ought to focus on the security and rebuilding of different biological systems that act as favorable places and transitory courses for birds.

Alleviation of Commotion Contamination:
Human-prompted commotion contamination represents a huge danger to bird melodies, particularly in metropolitan and rural conditions. Alleviating commotion contamination through metropolitan preparation, green framework, and sound walls can make spaces where avian correspondence can prosper. Safeguarding regular soundscapes adds to the prosperity of bird populaces and the natural equilibrium of territories.

Checking and Preservation of Compromised Species:
Bird melodies act as significant marks of the soundness of bird populaces. Checking changes in vocal way of behaving can assist with recognizing dangers to species and biological systems, giving early alerts of natural debasement or environment misfortune. Preservation techniques can then be created to address explicit difficulties and safeguard weak bird species.

Instruction and Mindfulness:
Expanding public mindfulness about the social and biological meaning of bird melodies is vital for cultivating a feeling of obligation toward avian preservation. Instructive projects, outreach drives, and local area commitment can add to a more extensive comprehension of the significance of saving regular soundscapes and the different vocalizations of bird species.

3.2 Relationship between Songs and Reproductive Behavior

In the huge orchestra of the regular world, melodies assume a significant part in the conceptive way of behaving of various species. From the sweet calls of birds to the musical croaking of frogs, the complicated tunes of the set of all animals are frequently unpredictably connected to the journey for mates, foundation of domains, and effective proliferation. This investigation digs into the entrancing connection among tunes and conceptive way of behaving, revealing the transformative importance, various techniques, and the significant job of vocalizations in the complex dance of romance and mating.

I. Developmental Meaning of Conceptive Tunes:
Mate Fascination and Choice:

Birds: In avian species, melodies are useful assets for mate fascination. Male birds frequently take part in intricate and species-explicit vocalizations to flag their presence, hereditary wellness, and regional ability to likely mates. The intricacy and energy of these melodies are frequently connected to the conceptive outcome of people, as females are known to normally like mates with additional mind boggling vocal collections.

Creatures of land and water: Frogs and amphibians additionally depend on vocalizations to draw in mates. Their calls, frequently unmistakable to every species, act as notices of their presence. Female frogs, outfitted with the capacity to observe explicit call attributes, utilize these vocalizations as signs to assess the hereditary wellness of expected mates.

Regional Safeguard:
Birds: Melodies are apparatuses for mate fascination as well as act as regional markers. Male birds use vocalizations to delineate and safeguard domains from rival guys. The foundation of domains is urgent for getting assets and drawing in expected mates, shaping an immediate connection between tunes, an area, and regenerative achievement.

Warm blooded animals: In vertebrates, for example, primates and large felines, vocalizations are utilized for both mate fascination and regional guard. Thundering in huge felines and complex vocalizations in primates impart predominance, regional limits, and regenerative wellness. Females might be attracted to guys with additional strong vocalizations, showing strength and energy.

II. Romance Customs and Vocal Presentations:
Avian Romance Presentations:

Larks: Romance showcases in warblers include many-sided vocalizations joined by actual developments, energetic plumage shows, and other viewable prompts. These presentations are basic to the romance cycle, cultivating pair holding and upgrading the probability of fruitful mating.

Waterfowl: Ducks and geese take part in synchronized vocalizations and presentations during romance. These vocalizations, frequently as synchronized calls, add to coordinate development and build up the connection between mates.

Land and water proficient Vocal Showcases:
Anurans: Anurans, which incorporate frogs and amphibians, are famous for their remarkable vocal showcases during romance. Male anurans produce species-explicit calls to draw in females. In certain species, synchronized chorales of guys can be heard, making an aggregate ensemble that improves the general engaging quality of a rearing site.

III. Correspondence in Friendly Well evolved creatures:
Primate Vocalizations:

Social Holding: Primates, being exceptionally friendly creatures, use vocalizations for different parts of social holding, including conceptive ways of behaving. Calls, for example, mating calls, sexual intercourse calls, and newborn child trouble calls reinforce social bonds inside primate gatherings.

Mate Monitoring: In some primate species, guys use vocalizations to watch mates from likely opponents. By expressing and showing their presence, guys stop different guys from moving toward females during basic conceptive periods.

Cetacean Melodies:
Whales and Dolphins: Cetaceans, like whales and dolphins, are known for their intricate vocalizations, frequently alluded to as tunes. These tunes assume a part in mate fascination and social union inside gatherings. In certain species, guys sing mind boggling melodies to draw in females, adding to the development of impermanent or long haul mating coalitions.

IV. Versatile Techniques and Sign Substance:
Fluctuation and Uniqueness:

Lark Changeability: Warblers display individual fluctuation in their vocalizations. This fluctuation, affected by hereditary qualities and learning, permits people to have interesting tunes, adding to mate acknowledgment and reinforcing pair bonds.

Land and water proficient Call Variety: Anurans frequently have different call collections, with individual guys delivering varieties of their species-explicit call. This variety can act as a type of individual distinguishing proof and may impact mate decision.

Learning and Social Transmission:

Lark Learning: Numerous warblers get familiar with their tunes during a basic time of improvement. Youthful birds get tunes through a blend of hereditary inclination and openness to grown-up conspecifics. Social transmission of tunes inside populaces prompts the arrangement of provincial vernaculars and exceptional vocal customs.

Primate Social Transmission: In primates, including extraordinary gorillas, vocalizations are learned ways of behaving went down through ages. The social transmission of vocalizations guarantees the congruity of explicit calls, incorporating those related with regenerative ways of behaving, inside gatherings.

V. Natural Effects on Regenerative Tunes:
Acoustic Variations:

Birdsong in Loud Conditions: Birds adjust their vocalizations to ecological circumstances. In metropolitan conditions with expanded commotion contamination, some bird species change the recurrence and timing of their tunes to be heard over foundation clamor. This variation guarantees powerful correspondence in testing acoustic conditions.

Frog Brings in Wetlands: Anuran calls are impacted by ecological elements, particularly in wetland environments. The acoustic properties of water impact the transmission of calls, prompting variations in call recurrence and span to improve correspondence in amphibian conditions.

VI. Human Effect and Preservation Suggestions:
Anthropogenic Commotion Contamination:

Disturbance of Correspondence: Human exercises, including urbanization and industrialization, present huge degrees of clamor contamination.

Raised commotion levels can disrupt regenerative correspondence in different species, influencing mate fascination, domain safeguard, and generally conceptive achievement.

Preservation Difficulties: The effect of anthropogenic commotion on regenerative tunes presents protection challenges. Endeavors to alleviate commotion contamination and protect regular soundscapes are pivotal for keeping up with viable conceptive correspondence in different environments.

Loss of Natural surroundings and Discontinuity:
Influence on Larks: Environment misfortune and fracture disturb the rearing living spaces of warblers, prompting decreases in populaces. The deficiency of appropriate domains and settling locales hampers the capacity of birds to take part in powerful regenerative correspondence.

Land and water proficient Decays: Anurans, especially those ward on unambiguous amphibian natural surroundings for reproducing, face declines because of living space misfortune and debasement. Conservation of wetland natural surroundings is fundamental for keeping up with the acoustic conditions important for fruitful regenerative correspondence.

3.3   Regional Variations in Birdsong

Birdsong, an ensemble that reverberations through different scenes, displays exceptional local varieties molded by natural variables, territory qualities, and, surprisingly, social impacts. From the melodic tunes of warblers in calm woods to the musical calls of tropical birds in rainforests, provincial varieties in birdsong paint a distinctive representation of the many-sided connections between avian networks and their surroundings. This investigation dives into the variables adding to territorial varieties in birdsong, the environmental meaning of these varieties, and the social aspects that further advance comprehension we might interpret avian correspondence.

Natural Elements Impacting Provincial Varieties:
Environment Attributes:
Various environments force particular acoustic difficulties and open doors for birds. The construction of vegetation, the presence of water bodies, and the geology of the scene all add to the acoustic climate. Birds adjust their vocalizations to these natural surroundings qualities, bringing about varieties in pitch, recurrence, and sufficiency. For example, birds in thick woodlands might create lower-recurrence tunes that help better through vegetation, while those in open environments might involve higher frequencies for successful correspondence.

Asset Accessibility:
The accessibility of assets, including food and settling destinations, impacts the vocal way of behaving of birds. In districts where assets are bountiful, birds might put more in complex tunes to draw in mates and lay out domains. Then again, in regions with restricted assets, birds might depend on less difficult vocalizations to pass on fundamental data. Provincial varieties in asset accessibility add to the variety of birdsong designs saw across various biological systems.

Environment and Occasional Changes:
Environment and occasional varieties assume a huge part in molding birdsong designs. In mild areas, where unmistakable seasons happen, birds change their vocalizations in light of reproducing seasons, relocation designs, and natural circumstances. The beginning of spring, for instance, frequently sets off an expansion in melody action as birds participate in romance and lay out domains. Provincial contrasts in environment and occasional cycles add to the worldly varieties in birdsong saw across various scopes.

Species Variety and Collaborations:
The presence of different bird species inside a district adds to an intricate snare of collaborations.
Various species might share natural surroundings, prompting interspecific contest for assets and space. Birds change their vocalizations to limit obstruction with different species, bringing about extraordinary provincial varieties. The piece of avian networks inside a particular region impacts the general acoustic scene and adds to the provincial subtleties of birdsong.

Geographic Elements:
Geographic highlights, like mountains, valleys, and waterways, can shape the proliferation of sound. Birds change their melodies to advance correspondence inside these geological requirements. The reverberations delivered in bumpy territory, for instance, may impact the construction of bird vocalizations. Moreover, the presence of water bodies can enhance or constrict sound, affecting the acoustic climate and prompting unmistakable territorial varieties in birdsong.

Social Impacts on Provincial Birdsongs:
Tongues and Social Transmission:
Birds, especially larks, display social transmission of vocalizations inside populaces. Like human tongues, birds in a specific district might foster particular lingos in their melodies. Youthful birds gain these local tongues from more seasoned, more

experienced people, making a social practice of vocal correspondence. This social part of birdsong adds to the rich embroidered artwork of local varieties inside species.

Social Learning and Impersonation:
Many birds are equipped for mimicking the sounds in their current circumstance, including the melodies of other bird species and, surprisingly, non-natural sounds. Social learning and impersonation add to the advancement of local vocal customs. In districts where explicit sounds or vocalizations are predominant, birds might integrate these components into their melodies, prompting one of a kind provincial varieties that are gone down through ages.

Urbanization and Anthropogenic Impact:
Human exercises, including urbanization and natural surroundings modification, can impact local birdsong designs. Metropolitan conditions present new sounds, for example, traffic and human-created commotion, which might affect the acoustic scene. A few birds adjust to these progressions by integrating metropolitan sounds into their melodies. Anthropogenic impacts, including the presentation of non-local species, can likewise add to shifts in territorial birdsong designs.

Social Practices and Imagery:
In specific societies, birds and their melodies hold representative importance. Customary practices, old stories, and social convictions might impact the insight and translation of bird vocalizations. Nearby people group might integrate birdsongs into social customs, narrating, or craftsmanship, further forming the social elements of territorial birdsong.

Instances of Local Varieties:
European Robin (Erithacus rubecula):
The European Robin, found across Europe, displays unmistakable local varieties in its melody. Birds in northern districts frequently produce more slow, lower-pitched melodies, while those in southern locales have quicker, sharp sounding tunes. These varieties are accepted to be affected by environmental elements, including temperature and natural surroundings structure.

Normal Songbird (Luscinia megarhynchos):
Songbirds are known for their strong and differed melodies. Various populaces of normal songbirds across Europe have been found to display provincial varieties in their

melodies. These varieties are viewed as social, with birds in unambiguous locales sharing normal melody designs.

Tune Sparrow (Melospiza melodia):
Melody Sparrows in North America are prestigious for their different collection of tunes. Local varieties in Melody Sparrow tunes have been archived, with unmistakable lingos saw in various populaces. These varieties are advanced socially, went down through ages inside nearby networks of birds.

Lyrebirds (Menura spp.):
The Eminent Lyrebird and different species in the variety Menura, local to Australia, are exceptional copies fit for emulating many sounds, including the calls of other bird species and mechanical clamors. Provincial varieties in lyrebird tunes might mirror the neighborhood soundscape and social impacts inside their living spaces.

Preservation Suggestions and Difficulties:
Understanding provincial varieties in birdsong is pivotal for protection endeavors, as movements in vocal examples might flag changes in biological systems and biodiversity.

Bioacoustic Observing:
Bioacoustic observing, utilizing mechanized recording gadgets and sound examination programming, permits scientists to follow local varieties in birdsong after some time. Checking changes in vocalizations can give important experiences into shifts in bird populaces, the effect of living space changes, and reactions to environment related variances.

Protection of Regular Soundscapes:
Safeguarding regular soundscapes is fundamental for keeping up with the respectability of territorial birdsong designs. Protection endeavors ought to focus on the safeguarding of different living spaces, limiting anthropogenic clamor contamination, and guaranteeing that environments stay helpful for the regular vocalizations of bird species.

Instruction and Effort:
Public mindfulness and training projects can assume a crucial part in encouraging appreciation for territorial varieties in birdsong. Outreach drives that feature the social and biological meaning of birdsongs can add to a more extensive comprehension of the significance of safeguarding avian biodiversity and normal soundscapes.

Territory Protection and Reclamation:

Territory protection and reclamation endeavors are central for keeping up with the circumstances that help provincial birdsong varieties. Safeguarding different natural surroundings, incorporating those with one of a kind geographic elements and vegetation structures, adds to the versatility of avian networks and their vocal customs.

Chapter 4:
Visual Signals and Body Language

Correspondence is a complex peculiarity, stretching out a long ways past the expressed word. Visual signals and non-verbal communication comprise a huge part of human connection, forming the manner in which we comprehend and answer each other. This extensive investigation digs into the complex universe of non-verbal correspondence, analyzing the subtleties of visual signals and non-verbal communication. From the developmental foundations of these correspondence modalities to their social varieties and contemporary importance, this talk expects to disentangle the quiet ensemble that assumes a urgent part in our everyday cooperations.

Presentation:

Correspondence is the backbone of human cooperation, and keeping in mind that words convey unequivocal implications, visual signals and non-verbal communication frequently say a lot peacefully. Understanding these non-verbal prompts is likened to interpreting an old content that conveys feelings, goals, and perspectives. This investigation looks to disentangle the layers of visual signals and non-verbal communication, revealing insight into their transformative starting points, social appearances, and functional applications in different settings.

Transformative Roots:

To appreciate the meaning of visual signals and non-verbal communication, following their developmental roots is basic. From the base tokens of our precursors to the complex non-verbal correspondence frameworks of current people, these signs have developed as versatile instruments. Early people depended intensely on non-verbal prompts to convey risk, express feelings, and lay out friendly ordered progressions. Understanding the transformative underpinnings gives an establishment to getting a handle on the inborn parts of non-verbal correspondence.

The Life structures of Non-verbal communication:

Non-verbal communication envelops a heap of components, including looks, signals, stance, and eye to eye connection. Every part adds to the rich embroidery of non-verbal correspondence, filling in as a reflection of our internal contemplations and sentiments.

Looks, for example, are an all inclusive language that rises above social limits, conveying feelings like satisfaction, bitterness, outrage, and shock. Inspecting the subtleties of various non-verbal communication components gives knowledge into the many-sided ways people communicate their thoughts without expressing a word.

Social Varieties:
While specific parts of non-verbal communication might be widespread, social varieties assume a vital part in forming non-verbal correspondence standards. What might be viewed as a considerate signal in one culture could be seen as hostile in another. This segment investigates the effect of social setting on visual signals and non-verbal communication, featuring the significance of social responsiveness in deciphering non-verbal prompts. Through contextual investigations and models, we dive into the complicated dance of signals and articulations across various social orders.

Social Elements:
Visual signals and non-verbal communication are dynamic devices that explore the mind boggling landscape of social associations. From the meeting room to the heartfelt supper table, non-verbal correspondence shapes the elements of connections. This segment researches the job of non-verbal communication in different social settings, analyzing how power elements, orientation jobs, and relational associations are impacted by non-verbal prompts. Understanding the implicit language of social elements enables people to explore these circumstances with increased mindfulness.

Double dealing and Truth:
Visual signals and non-verbal communication can be both uncovering and misleading. While certifiable feelings frequently manifest through non-verbal signals, people may likewise utilize intentional motions to cover their actual sentiments. This part digs into the complexities of double dealing and truth in non-verbal communication, investigating the study of identifying lies through unpretentious signals. Unwinding the secret of non-verbal duplicity upgrades our capacity to explore the almost negligible difference among truthfulness and façade.

Useful Applications:
Past relational elements, visual signals and non-verbal communication track down commonsense applications in assorted fields. From business talks to criminal examinations, experts across disciplines tackle the force of non-verbal correspondence. This segment investigates the commonsense utilizations of non-verbal communication in different settings, underscoring its part in viable authority, compromise, and fruitful correspondence procedures.

Innovative Progressions:
In the computerized age, where eye to eye collaborations are frequently intervened by screens, the scene of visual signals and non-verbal communication is developing. Video conferencing, augmented reality, and different innovations acquaint new aspects with non-verbal correspondence. This segment inspects the effect of mechanical headways on the articulation and translation of non-verbal communication, taking into account both the valuable open doors and difficulties introduced by these advancements.

4.1 Display Behaviors for Courtship and Mating

The perplexing dance of romance and mating in the animals of the world collectively is in many cases joined by a stunning cluster of show ways of behaving. These ways of behaving, going from intricate customs to lively visual signs, assume a critical part in the choice of mates and the continuation of species. This investigation digs into the entrancing universe of show ways of behaving, disentangling their developmental starting points, variety across species, and the complicated exchange among structure and capability chasing conceptive achievement.

Presentation:
Romance and mating ways of behaving are central parts of regenerative systems across the set of all animals. Show ways of behaving, specifically, are the visual and social signals that people utilize to draw in and evaluate expected mates. From the showy showcases of birds of heaven to the inconspicuous moves of bugs, these ways of behaving are a demonstration of the transformative tensions that have molded them. This investigation looks to reveal the different elements of show ways of behaving with regards to romance and mating, revealing insight into their versatile importance and the variety they bring to the domain of regenerative procedures.

Transformative Beginnings:
To comprehend the meaning of show ways of behaving in romance and mating, it is vital to dig into their developmental starting points. These ways of behaving have arisen as systems to improve conceptive accomplishment by expanding the possibilities of effective mate determination. From the energetic plumage of birds to the multifaceted romance moves of vertebrates, show ways of behaving have advanced as variations to ecological difficulties and social elements. This segment investigates the underlying foundations of show ways of behaving, following their development as instruments for drawing in mates, laying out predominance, and guaranteeing effective generation.

Variety Across Species:
Show ways of behaving are surprisingly assorted, mirroring the bunch manners by which various species have adjusted to their natural specialties. This part gives a relative examination of show ways of behaving across different scientific categorizations, featuring the scope of methodologies utilized by creatures chasing romance and mating. From the entrancing presentations of marine animals to the mind boggling romance customs of vertebrates, the variety of show ways of behaving grandstands the imagination of development in molding conceptive methodologies.

Visual Signs and Shading:
One noticeable classification of show ways of behaving includes visual signs and hue. Numerous species influence distinctive varieties, examples, and showcases to draw in mates. Peacocks, for instance, grandstand their intricate and radiant plumage during romance presentations. Also, butterflies take part in ethereal gymnastics, uncovering their energetic wings to possible mates. This part investigates the job of visual signs and hue in romance, analyzing how these presentations act as genuine marks of hereditary wellness, wellbeing, and the capacity to put resources into propagation.

Romance Ceremonies and Moves:
Past visual signs, romance frequently includes perplexing customs and moves. From the synchronized showcases of avian two part harmonies to the intricate romance moves of warm blooded animals, these ways of behaving are arranged articulations of interest and similarity. The segment analyzes the capability of romance customs, taking into account how they add to mate choice, build up pair bonds, and lay out the similarity of likely mates. Contextual analyses of species with prominent romance customs offer experiences into the job of these ways of behaving in conceptive achievement.

Hear-able Showcases:
While visual signs assume an unmistakable part in romance showcases, hear-able signals likewise highlight noticeably in the conceptive collection of numerous species. From the melodic tunes of birds to the thunderous calls of creatures of land and water, sound fills in as a strong mechanism for correspondence during romance. This segment investigates the job of hear-able showcases in mate fascination, correspondence between possible mates, and the foundation of domains. The variety of sounds and their versatile importance in various conditions give a rich embroidery of hear-able romance ways of behaving.

Systems of Sexual Determination:

Show ways of behaving are frequently complicatedly connected to the idea of sexual choice, where people with specific qualities or ways of behaving have a higher probability of conceptive achievement. This segment dives into the systems of sexual determination driven by show ways of behaving, including female decision, male rivalry, and the job of these ways of behaving in the advancement of optional sexual attributes. Understanding the elements of sexual choice reveals insight into the developmental powers that shape the variety of show ways of behaving saw in the normal world.

Human Romance:

While frequently connected with the collective of animals, show ways of behaving likewise manifest in human romance. In spite of the fact that our strategies might contrast from those of our non-human partners, people participate in an assortment of show ways of behaving to draw in and survey possible mates. This segment investigates the job of non-verbal communication, preparing, and other visual signs in human romance, taking into account the social and cultural impacts that shape these ways of behaving. The equals and qualifications among human and creature romance ways of behaving give important experiences into the comprehensiveness and changeability of show procedures.

Preservation Suggestions:

As human exercises progressively influence normal living spaces, the investigation of show ways of behaving takes on added importance for protection endeavors. Numerous species depend on unambiguous natural signals and conditions for fruitful romance and mating. Human-incited changes to environments, including territory annihilation and environmental change, can disturb these basic ways of behaving, possibly imperiling species endurance. This segment examines the preservation ramifications of understanding and saving the assorted presentation ways of behaving that add to conceptive achievement and biodiversity.

4.2   Non-vocal Communication Methods

Correspondence is a powerful interaction of words, signals, and articulations, reaching out past vocalization. Non-vocal specialized strategies assume a vital part in conveying contemplations, feelings, and goals without the requirement for verbally expressed words. From looks to non-verbal communication, this investigation digs into the different and nuanced domain of non-vocal correspondence, revealing insight into its importance, social varieties, and reasonable applications across different settings.

Looks:

Looks act as a widespread language, rising above phonetic obstructions to convey a range of feelings. The human face is fit for creating a horde of looks, from a veritable grin to a wrinkled temple of concern. Every facial muscle development conveys unobtrusive subtleties that add profundity and setting to our connections. This part investigates the job of looks in non-vocal correspondence, underlining the significance of understanding the prompts implanted in grins, glares, and the endless articulations that shape our everyday associations.

Non-verbal communication:

The body is a material of non-verbal correspondence, with developments and stances passing on an abundance of data. From the sure step of a pioneer to the slumped stance of somebody feeling crushed, non-verbal communication conveys volumes around one's feelings and outlook. This segment digs into the complexities of non-verbal communication, looking at the manners by which signals, stance, and developments add to the quiet exchange between people. Understanding non-verbal communication improves relational correspondence by giving experiences into implicit considerations and sentiments.

Motions and Gesture based communication:

Motions, both unconstrained and socially imbued, structure a critical part of non-vocal correspondence. Whether it's a flood of the hand, a thumbs up, or more intricate communication through signing frameworks, signals convey meaning effectively and frequently with social particularity. This segment investigates the rich variety of motions and gesture based communication, featuring their part in crossing over correspondence holes, particularly in settings where vocalization might be restricted or unrealistic.

Proxemics:

The investigation of proxemics centers around the utilization of individual space in correspondence. The distance between people during an association can convey closeness, custom, or distress. Proxemics stretches out past actual closeness to incorporate territoriality and the control of room to impact correspondence elements. This segment looks at how people use and decipher individual space, revealing insight into the implicit principles that oversee our collaborations and connections.

Contact and Haptics:

Contact is a strong non-vocal specialized strategy that can communicate solace, backing, or even pass on messages of power. Haptics, the investigation of touch, envelops a great many material connections, from a consoling gesture of congratulations to a strong handshake.

This part investigates the social varieties in the translation of touch and the job of haptics in laying out associations, cultivating trust, and conveying a range of feelings.

Eye to eye connection:
The eyes are frequently alluded to as the windows to the spirit, and eye to eye connection is an intense non-vocal specialized strategy. It can communicate truthfulness, certainty, or even convey a feeling of weakness. This part dives into the nuanced job of eye to eye connection in correspondence, investigating its social varieties and the effect it has on the apparent earnestness and commitment of people in a discussion.

Social Varieties in Non-Vocal Correspondence:
The translation of non-vocal specialized strategies isn't all around predictable yet is impacted by social standards and practices. What might be viewed as a satisfactory signal in one culture may be seen as hostile in another. This segment investigates the social varieties in non-vocal correspondence, stressing the significance of social awareness in understanding and exploring the quiet language that underlies human association.

Viable Applications in Different Settings:
Non-vocal specialized strategies track down functional applications in a heap of settings. From business discussions and influential positions to medical services settings and relational connections, the compelling use and understanding of non-vocal signals can fundamentally affect results. This part analyzes the pragmatic utilizations of non-vocal specialized techniques, giving bits of knowledge into how people can use these prompts for progress in assorted proficient and individual circumstances.

Difficulties and Misinterpretations:
While non-vocal correspondence is an incredible asset, it isn't without its difficulties. Misinterpretations can happen when social standards conflict, or when people misread signals because of individual predispositions. This segment investigates the likely difficulties and entanglements related with non-vocal correspondence, underscoring the requirement for mindfulness, sympathy, and liberality to cultivate successful correspondence.

4.3   Role of Plumage and Gestures in Avian Interaction

Avian correspondence is a spellbinding orchestra of viewable prompts and motions, with plumage and body developments assuming crucial parts. For birds, the lively exhibit of quills and arranged motions act as a language that rises above the limits of vocalization.

This investigation dives into the unpredictable universe of avian association, unwinding the meaning of plumage and motions in correspondence, mate choice, and the foundation of social ordered progressions.

Plumage: A Range of Articulation:
The plumage of birds is a work of art of nature's creativity, filling both functional and open needs. Feathers give protection, help in flight, and safeguard against natural components. In any case, they likewise assume a significant part in avian correspondence. This segment dives into the multi-layered nature of plumage, investigating how tones, examples, and presentations add to the correspondence techniques of birds.

Tinge and Flagging:
Birds display a surprising variety of plumage tones, each filling a particular need in correspondence. From the radiant shades of hummingbirds to the striking examples of birds of heaven, hue is a strong visual sign. This segment looks at the job of plumage shading in avian correspondence, taking into account how it works with mate fascination, lays out regional limits, and conveys strength inside an animal categories.

Shedding and Occasional Changes:
The unique idea of plumage reaches out past static tones and examples. Birds go through shedding, an interaction that includes the shedding and substitution of plumes. Shedding, frequently synchronized with occasional changes, impacts the presence of birds and can flag different life stages, for example, development or status to raise. Understanding the recurrent idea of shedding gives experiences into the worldly parts of avian correspondence and conduct.

Romance Shows: The Expressive dance of Adoration:
Romance presentations are intricate movements that feature the excellence and essentialness of plumage. Male birds, specifically, frequently take part in unpredictable presentations to draw in possible mates. This part investigates the assorted romance showcases saw in various bird species, from the synchronized moves of cranes to the ethereal trapeze artistry of birds like the wonderful lyrebird. These presentations are outwardly staggering as well as act as urgent components in mate choice.

Disguise and Secretive Shading:
While certain birds use plumage to stick out, others utilize it as a type of disguise. Obscure tinge and cover permit birds to mix consistently into their environmental factors, giving insurance from hunters.

This part explores the versatile meaning of obscure plumage, featuring how it supports endurance by limiting perceivability and expanding the possibilities of fruitful searching and settling.

Signals in Avian Association:
Past plumage, avian correspondence includes a collection of signals and developments. Birds use non-verbal communication to convey expectations, lay out strength, and explore social elements. This part investigates the meaning of motions in avian collaboration, revealing insight into how developments add to the complex non-vocal correspondence among birds.

Acts and Ritualized Developments:
Birds impart through various stances and ritualized developments that pass on unambiguous messages. From the head-swaying of pigeons to the wing-spreading showcases of flying predators, these motions are fundamental to laying out domains, drawing in mates, and conveying inside gatherings. Looking at the nuanced implications behind these stances gives a window into the rich universe of avian connection.

Agonistic Showcases:
In circumstances of contention or rivalry, birds participate in agonistic showcases that effectively stop matches and attest predominance. These presentations might include forceful stances, vocalizations, and misrepresented developments. Understanding the language of agonistic presentations is vital for interpreting the social orders and regional limits inside bird networks.

Parental Ways of behaving and Correspondence:
Parental consideration and correspondence are fundamental parts of avian way of behaving. Settling birds utilize different motions and motions toward speak with their mates and posterity. From the trading of taking care of obligations to advance notice signals within the sight of hunters, avian guardians utilize a blend of plumage shows and motions to guarantee the endurance of their descendants.

Species-Explicit Correspondence:
Different bird species have advanced interesting correspondence systems customized to their biological specialties and social designs. This segment investigates a choice of eminent models, from the unpredictable mimicry of lyrebirds to the synchronized trips of starlings known as murmurations. Understanding species-explicit correspondence improves our appreciation for the variety of avian communications and variations.

Chapter 5:
The Secret Life of Bird Calls

Birds, with their dynamic plumage and effortless flights, have consistently caught the human creative mind. In any case, past their visual quality lies a secret world that frequently slips through the cracks — the complicated and entrancing domain of bird calls. The mysterious existence of bird calls is an ensemble of nature, a complicated language that fills a horde of needs in the avian world. This article digs into the profundities of this hear-able woven artwork, investigating the science, variety, and meaning of bird brings in the existences of our padded friends.

The Study of Bird Calls
1. Vocal Life structures
To comprehend the mysterious existence of bird calls, we should initially investigate the science behind these melodic expressions. Birds, in contrast to vertebrates, need vocal strings. All things being equal, they produce sounds utilizing a specific vocal organ called the syrinx. Situated at the foundation of the windpipe where it parts into the bronchi, the syrinx considers an unrivaled variety of sounds. The complicated command over the syrinx muscles empowers birds to tweak pitch, volume, and even produce different notes all the while.

2. Correspondence Purposes
Bird calls fill a huge number of needs, going from correspondence to regional safeguard and romance ceremonies. The intricacy and assortment of these calls are molded by developmental tensions and the particular requirements of every species. A few birds have exceptionally evolved collections, while others depend on a couple of particular calls to pass on data inside their gatherings.

The Variety of Bird Calls
1. Species-Explicit Calls
Each bird species has an exceptional arrangement of calls that recognize it from others. These species-explicit calls assume a critical part in correspondence inside the local area, assisting people with remembering each other and supporting social bonds. For example, the hauntingly wonderful tune of the thrush or the bright twitters of sparrows are undeniable marks of their individual species.

2. Mimicry and Impersonation

Mimicry is one more entrancing part of bird calls. An animal varieties have the striking skill to emulate the calls of different birds, creatures, or even human-uttered sounds. The lyrebird of Australia, eminent for its amazing mimicry abilities, integrates the hints of trimming tools and camera screens into its collection. This capacity isn't just for diversion; it frequently fills pragmatic needs like confounding hunters or drawing in mates.

The Usefulness of Bird Calls
1. Domain Stamping

One of the essential elements of bird calls is the boundary of domains. Male birds, specifically, utilize their vocal ability to lay out and protect their turf. The redundant and particular nature of regional calls fills in as an unmistakable advance notice to gatecrashers, assisting with forestalling clashes and keep social control inside bird networks.

2. Romance Ceremonies

Bird calls assume a urgent part in romance ceremonies. Male birds frequently utilize intricate and musical melodies to draw in possible mates. The intricacy of these tunes isn't only for tasteful allure; it passes on data about the artist's wellbeing, hereditary wellness, and capacity to accommodate posterity. Female birds, thusly, evaluate these characteristics while choosing a mate.

3. Caution Calls

Birds are profoundly sensitive to their environmental elements, and their calls can go about as an early advance notice framework. Caution calls effectively ready others in the group or local area about expected dangers, going from hunters to antagonistic atmospheric conditions. The explicitness of these calls might show the sort of risk, considering composed reactions inside the gathering.

The Social Meaning of Bird Calls
1. Legends and Imagery

Over the entire course of time, bird calls have held social importance in different social orders. They highlight unmistakably in legends, frequently representing different ideas like love, opportunity, or looming occasions. The eerie call of the crackpot, for instance, has enlivened fantasies and stories in native societies, while the songbird's tune has been an image of magnificence and yearning in Western writing.

2. Birdwatching and Ecotourism

Birdwatching, the perception of birds right at home, has turned into a well known sporting movement. Aficionados and ornithologists the same listen distinctly to bird calls as they recognize and record various species. The variety of bird calls adds a hear-able aspect to the experience, upgrading the enthusiasm for the regular world and adding to the developing field of ecotourism.

Preservation Suggestions
1. Bioacoustics in Protection

The investigation of bird calls, known as bioacoustics, has turned into an important device in preservation endeavors. Scientists use sound accounts to screen bird populaces, survey biodiversity, and track changes in environments. The vanishing or modification of explicit calls can flag ecological aggravations, giving early signs of territory corruption or environmental change influences.

2. Human-Incited Commotion Contamination

As urbanization spreads and human exercises infringe upon normal territories, birds face new difficulties. Human-incited clamor contamination, from traffic to modern apparatus, can impede bird correspondence. A few animal groups might change their brings to be heard over the noise, while others might endure disturbances in essential exercises like mating and taking care of. Understanding these elements is pivotal for moderating the effect of human exercises on avian networks.

Future Bearings in Bird Call Exploration
1. Mechanical Advances

Progressions in innovation, including man-made consciousness and AI, are altering the investigation of bird calls. Mechanized frameworks can now dissect immense measures of sound information, supporting analysts in recording species, observing populaces, and acquiring bits of knowledge into the social nature of birds. These instruments open new outskirts for grasping the intricacies of avian correspondence.

2. Environmental Change and Social Transformations

Environmental change represents a huge danger to biodiversity, and bird populaces are not excluded. Concentrating on how bird calls might change in light of moving natural circumstances can give significant data about species flexibility. Scientists are investigating whether birds modify their brings in recurrence, term, or example as a reaction to environment related changes, offering a remarkable viewpoint on the natural effects of an Earth-wide temperature boost.

5.1   Cryptic Communication and Alarm Calls

The avian world is a domain of perplexing correspondence, where birds utilize different signs to pass on data crucial for their endurance. Among the different types of avian correspondence, enigmatic correspondence and caution calls stand apart as urgent components in the perplexing woven artwork of bird connections. This article investigates the entrancing domains of enigmatic correspondence and caution calls, revealing insight into the components, capabilities, and natural meaning of these avian ways of behaving.

Mysterious Correspondence: The Specialty of Covering

1. Definition and Components

Mysterious correspondence alludes to the unobtrusive and frequently covered manners by which birds pass data on to each other, principally to stay away from discovery by hunters or adversaries. Dissimilar to the prominent and musical melodies related with romance or regional showcases, secretive correspondence works on a more clandestine level. Birds utilize a scope of visual, olfactory, and hear-able techniques to impart without drawing unnecessary consideration.

2. Plumage and Disguise

One of the most outwardly striking parts of secretive correspondence is the utilization of plumage for disguise. Many bird species have advanced shading and examples that permit them to mix flawlessly into their regular environmental elements. This fills the double need of keeping away from hunters and working with secretive methodologies during hunting or searching exercises. Models incorporate the enigmatic plumage of owls, which empowers them to turn out to be almost undetectable against tree husk or foliage.

3. Unobtrusive Non-verbal communication

Notwithstanding obvious signs, birds use unobtrusive non-verbal communication to speak with conspecifics and likely dangers. This can include slight developments, pose changes, or even the utilization of explicit motions that pass on data without drawing in the consideration of hunters or contenders. Noticing these subtleties requires a sharp eye, as they are frequently intangible to the easygoing onlooker.

Caution Calls: A Quick Reaction Framework

1. Transformative Beginnings

Caution calls are a basic part of avian correspondence, filling in as a fast reaction framework to expected dangers. The developmental starting points of alert gets back to can be followed to the requirement for early recognition of hunters, permitting birds to make a sly move and safeguard themselves, their homes, and their posterity.

This endurance component has been tweaked over ages, bringing about a different cluster of caution calls across various species.

2. Kinds of Alert Calls

Alert calls are surprisingly different, going from straightforward, piercing notes to complex arrangements of sounds. Various sorts of caution calls might pass on unambiguous data about the idea of the danger, for example, the presence of a ground hunter versus a flying one. Some caution calls are general and might be utilized for various dangers, while others are profoundly unambiguous, showing an exact kind of risk.

3. Social Transmission

The adequacy of alert calls lies in their nearby reaction as well as in their social transmission. At the point when one bird identifies a danger and issues a caution call, close by conspecifics rapidly get on the sign. This makes a cascading type of influence, with the whole rush or local area becoming mindful of the risk. The social idea of caution calls improves the aggregate capacity of a gathering to answer quickly and really to expected dangers.

Capabilities and Importance
1. Predation Hazard Evaluation

Obscure correspondence and alert calls assume vital parts in surveying and relieving predation chances. Obscure correspondence permits birds to move covertly through their surroundings, decreasing the probability of recognition by hunters. Then again, caution calls act as an early advance notice framework, giving birds the data expected to make a shifty move, stow away, or crowd potential dangers on the whole.

2. Facilitated Reactions

One of the striking parts of alert calls is their job in organizing aggregate reactions inside bird networks. At the point when a singular issues a caution call, it sets off a synchronized response among conspecifics. This might include the whole rush taking off, looking for cover, or participating in mobbing conduct to drive away a possible hunter. The planned idea of these reactions upgrades the possibilities of endurance for individual birds and the gathering in general.

3. Phony problems and Data Dependability

While caution calls are for the most part solid marks of risk, birds additionally face the test of knowing between genuine dangers and misleading problems. Deceptions might happen because of elements like misidentification, ecological aggravations, or the presence of non-ruthless substances.

The capacity of birds to separate between authentic dangers and phony problems is critical for advancing their reactions and staying away from pointless disturbances to ordinary exercises.

Contextual investigations: Prominent Instances of Enigmatic Correspondence and Alert Calls
1. Ground Settling Birds
Ground settling birds, like plovers and sandpipers, embody the utilization of obscure correspondence to cover their homes and eggs. These species frequently have enigmatically hued eggs that mix into the encompassing substrate, lessening the probability of location by outwardly arranged hunters. Furthermore, these birds might utilize interruption shows or pretend injury to redirect consideration from the home, utilizing obscure correspondence methodologies to safeguard their weak posterity.

2. Mobbing Conduct in Corvids
Corvids, including crows and jays, are known for their exceptionally evolved social designs and complex correspondence frameworks. At the point when a potential hunter is distinguished, a corvid will give an uproarious and particular caution call, alarming close by conspecifics. Accordingly, other corvids in the area might take part in mobbing conduct, all in all hassling and heading out the gatecrasher. This organized reaction is a demonstration of the viability of caution brings in advancing gathering protection.

3. Meerkats: Sentinel Conduct
While not birds, meerkats give a fascinating illustration of secretive correspondence and caution brings in a social mammalian animal types. Meerkats live in helpful gatherings and show sentinel conduct, where at least one people assume the job of saving watch for hunters. At the point when a sentinel recognizes a danger, it gives a particular caution call, flagging the whole gathering to seek shelter. This conduct shows the significance of correspondence in organizing against hunter techniques inside creature social orders.

Preservation Suggestions and Human Connections
1. Human-Actuated Unsettling influences
As human exercises infringe upon regular territories, birds face new difficulties connected with obscure correspondence and caution calls. Urbanization, deforestation, and sporting exercises can upset the inconspicuous correspondence techniques utilized by birds to keep away from hunters or opponents. Also, clamor contamination might impede the viability of alert calls, making it challenging for birds to distinguish and answer expected dangers.

2. Preservation Techniques

Understanding the complexities of mysterious correspondence and caution calls is significant for creating compelling protection methodologies. Saving regular territories, limiting human aggravations, and making cradle zones around basic reproducing and scrounging regions can assist with protecting the correspondence systems that are fundamental for bird endurance. Preservation endeavors ought to likewise consider the environmental significance of keeping up with solid populaces of birds that add to bother control, seed dispersal, and in general biological system balance.

Future Bearings in Exploration
1. Mechanical Advances in Bioacoustics

Headways in innovation, especially in the field of bioacoustics, offer new open doors for concentrating on mysterious correspondence and caution calls. Robotized recording frameworks, combined with AI calculations, can break down tremendous measures of sound information, permitting specialists to distinguish unobtrusive correspondence flags that might be impalpable to the human ear. This innovation holds guarantee for uncovering already obscure parts of avian correspondence techniques.

2. Joining of Social Biology and Physiology

Future examination ought to intend to coordinate social environment with physiological investigations to acquire a complete comprehension of how birds see and answer secretive correspondence and caution calls. Examining the brain and hormonal components engaged with handling and answering these signs can give experiences into the versatile meaning of these ways of behaving and their transformative underpinnings.

5.2   Hidden Messages in Short and Simple Calls

The avian world is a domain of multifaceted correspondence, where birds pass an abundance of data on through a different scope of calls. While some bird species are known for their intricate melodies, others depend on short and basic calls that convey stowed away messages. This article digs into the entrancing universe of these compact avian expressions, investigating the components, capabilities, and transformative meaning of stowed away messages in short and basic bird calls.

The Science Behind Short and Basic Calls
1. Vocal Life systems and Call Creation

Dissimilar to the pleasant tunes that frequently catch human consideration, short and basic calls are portrayed by their curtness and unequivocal quality. Understanding the science behind these calls requires a more critical glance at avian vocal life structures.

Birds produce sounds utilizing a particular vocal organ called the syrinx, and the compact idea of short calls is much of the time a consequence of exact muscle command over this organ. The straightforwardness of these calls misrepresents the intricacy of the basic physiological cycles.

2. Transformative Points of view

The development of short and straightforward calls is formed by the natural specialties and social designs of every species. These calls might have started as essential alert signs, considering quick correspondence in light of prompt dangers. Over the long haul, they might have broadened to pass nuanced data related on to scrounging, mating, and different parts of avian life. Researching the transformative starting points gives experiences into the versatile benefits gave by these brief specialized devices.

Elements of Short and Straightforward Calls
1. Caution Calls and Predation Evasion

One essential capability of short and basic calls is to make people inside a bird local area aware of expected dangers. These caution calls act as fast reaction systems, permitting birds to make a hesitant move and stay away from predation. The explicitness and criticalness of these calls can change, giving data about the presence of a danger as well as its temperament and closeness.

2. Scrounging Productivity

Short and straightforward calls likewise assume a part in planning searching exercises inside bird rushes. Birds might utilize particular calls to flag the revelation of food sources or to impart about the kind of food accessible. These short messages add to the effectiveness of gathering scavenging and can prompt a more fruitful double-dealing of assets.

3. Social Elements

Past prompt dangers and rummaging, short and straightforward calls add to the upkeep of social elements inside bird networks. They can pass on data about the presence of conspecifics, support social bonds, or sign regional limits. The brief idea of these calls takes into consideration speedy trades that are fundamental for exploring the intricacies of avian social orders.

Secret Messages: Unraveling the Importance
1. Variety in Pitch and Tone

While short and basic, bird calls frequently contain unpretentious varieties in pitch and tone that pass on extra data. These subtleties might flag profound states, like fervor, dread, or animosity. Translating these secret messages requires cautious perception and a comprehension of the setting in which the calls are delivered.

2. Logical Correspondence

Short and straightforward calls gain profundity through logical correspondence. A similar essential call might convey various implications relying upon the circumstance. For instance, a specific call could act as a caution within the sight of a hunter yet change into a searching sign when coordinated towards a food source. Analyzing the more extensive setting gives pivotal insights for unwinding the secret messages implanted in these brief calls.

Contextual investigations: Models from the Avian World
1. Chick-Help Brings in Pioneer Settling Birds

Pioneer settling birds, like terns and gulls, are known for their short and straightforward "chick-help" calls. These calls, produced by chicks in trouble, trigger fast and designated reactions from adjacent grown-ups. The grown-ups can recognize their own chick's call in the midst of a chaos of comparable sounds, showing the explicitness and acknowledgment capacities intrinsic in short and basic avian correspondence.

2. Sparrow Trills: Social Flagging

Sparrows, with their universal presence in metropolitan and provincial conditions, utilize short and basic requires different social purposes. Trills and tweets among sparrows act as good tidings, alarms, and signs of regional limits. The capacity to pass nuanced social data on through these concise calls adds to the flexibility and progress of sparrows in different living spaces.

3. Penguin Vocalizations: Social Union

In the chilly spreads of Antarctica, penguins depend on short and basic vocalizations to keep up with social union inside states. These calls work with correspondence between mates, guardians, and chicks. Penguins utilize particular calls to find each other in jam-packed states, exhibiting how compact correspondence is fundamental for exploring the difficulties of public living in unforgiving conditions.

Natural Importance and Protection Suggestions
1. Environment Wellbeing Pointers

The investigation of short and straightforward calls goes past the domain of ornithology, offering experiences into biological system wellbeing. Changes in the recurrence or example of these calls can act as early signs of ecological aggravations, living space debasement, or the presence of poisons. Observing avian correspondence can subsequently add to more extensive protection endeavors pointed toward safeguarding biodiversity.

2. Human-Actuated Effects

Human exercises, including urbanization, living space annihilation, and environmental change, can significantly affect the correspondence examples of birds. Short and basic calls, as delicate signs of ecological changes, might be dependent upon interruptions. Understanding the effect of human-incited changes on avian correspondence is pivotal for creating protection methodologies that moderate adverse consequences on bird populaces.

Innovative Advances and Future Exploration
1. Bioacoustics and Robotized Observing

Mechanical advances in bioacoustics and robotized observing frameworks have reformed the investigation of avian correspondence. Specialists presently utilize refined recording gadgets and AI calculations to investigate immense measures of sound information. These instruments empower the listing of various short and straightforward calls, giving a more extensive comprehension of the variety and elements of these vocalizations across bird species.

2. Incorporating Social Environment and Mental Science

Future examination headings include the coordination of conduct biology with mental science to dig further into the mental cycles basic short and straightforward calls. Exploring how birds see, process, and answer these calls can disclose the complexities of avian discernment. Understanding the mental parts of correspondence adds to our more extensive comprehension of creature knowledge and versatile ways of behaving.

5.3   Studying Bird Conversations in the Wild

In the tremendous span of the normal world, the skies are buzzing with the sweet orchestra of bird discussions. These avian trades, frequently inconspicuous and complex, act for of correspondence, including a bunch of messages from romance calls to regional alerts. Concentrating on bird discussions in the wild offers a dazzling look into the complicated language of our padded partners, disentangling the secrets of their social designs, biological jobs, and developmental transformations.

The Study of Bird Correspondence
Vocal Collection

Birds impart through a different cluster of vocalizations, each filling a particular need inside their social and environmental settings. The vocal collection of a bird animal varieties can incorporate tunes, calls, and different sounds, with each kind of vocalization conveying exceptional data. Melodies are frequently connected with romance and mating, while calls satisfy works like making aware of hunters, organizing with mates, and keeping up with bunch attachment.

Significance of Setting

Understanding bird discussions requires an appreciation for setting. A solitary call might have various implications relying upon the circumstance — whether it's an admonition of risk, an encouragement to mate, or a sign of food revelation. Noticing the general climate, the way of behaving of the birds, and the hour of day gives urgent setting to deciphering the messages implanted in their vocalizations.

Field Procedures for Concentrating on Bird Discussions
Bioacoustics

Bioacoustics is a principal device in the investigation of bird discussions. Analysts utilize specific hardware, like receivers and recorders, to catch and break down avian vocalizations. Propels in innovation, including robotized recording gadgets and PC calculations, empower the assortment of enormous datasets and the ID of explicit calls. Bioacoustic studies contribute not exclusively to figuring out the variety of bird vocalizations yet additionally to observing changes in bird populaces over the long haul.

Observational Examinations

Field ornithologists frequently utilize observational examinations to supplement bioacoustic research. Via cautiously watching and recording bird conduct, scientists can associate vocalizations with explicit exercises, assisting with translating the implications behind the calls. This active methodology permits researchers to catch the subtleties of bird discussions that might be missed in sound accounts alone.

Resident Science

Drawing in resident researchers in bird discussion studies has become progressively well known. With the assistance of birdwatchers and devotees, analysts can gather significant information on bird vocalizations across various areas and seasons. Resident science projects add to enormous scope studies, giving experiences into geological varieties in bird discussions and empowering analysts to follow long haul patterns.

Kinds of Bird Discussions
1. Tunes: The Language of Adoration

Bird tunes are frequently connected with romance and mating ceremonies. Male birds, specifically, utilize intricate and resonant melodies to draw in females and lay out domain. The intricacy and variety of melodies can fluctuate generally between species, exhibiting the one of a kind vocal marks that add to regenerative achievement.

2. Calls: Past the Tune

Not at all like melodies, calls are commonly more limited and serve a more extensive scope of capabilities. Caution calls, for instance, are quick and extreme, flagging expected dangers and setting off prompt reactions inside bird networks.

Contact calls assist with keeping up with union inside runs, permitting people to remain associated while searching or exploring through their current circumstance.

3. Duetting: Amicable Associations
In some bird species, especially among monogamous matches, duetting is a surprising type of correspondence. Mates take part in composed vocalizations, delivering an agreeable two part harmony that fortifies their bond and builds up their regional cases. Duetting serves for of correspondence as well as a presentation of organization and participation.

Social Elements and Regional Correspondence
1. Regional Guard
Birds use vocalizations to affirm and guard their regions. Regional calls act as an unmistakable advance notice to gatecrashers, flagging the limits of a bird's space. This regional correspondence forestalls clashes and lays out a progressive system inside bird networks.

2. Social Bonds
Bird discussions are fundamental for keeping up with social securities inside rushes or networks. Contact calls, delicate chatting, and other social vocalizations add to the union of bird gatherings. These communications are pivotal for facilitated exercises like rummaging, perching, and exploring through their environmental elements.

Contextual analyses: Instances of Bird Discussions
1. Mockingbirds: Mimicry as Correspondence
Mockingbirds are eminent for their uncommon mimicry abilities. They consolidate a great many sounds, including those of other bird species, bugs, and, surprisingly, human-made clamors, into their collection. Mimicry fills in as a type of correspondence, permitting mockingbirds to flag their versatility, dazzle expected mates, and lay out their presence inside a different acoustic scene.

2. Lyrebirds: Symphonies of the Backwoods
The sublime lyrebird of Australia is an expert of perplexing and elaborate melodies. Male lyrebirds make complex organizations by emulating the hints of other bird species, as well as components of their indigenous habitat. These virtuoso exhibitions assume a urgent part in drawing in females and getting mating potential open doors, displaying the nearby association between bird correspondence and conceptive achievement.

Protection Suggestions
1. Bioindicators of Biological system Wellbeing
Concentrating on bird discussions in the wild can give important bits of knowledge into the strength of environments. Changes in vocalization examples might show shifts in bird populaces, dispersion, or living space quality. Birds, as bioindicators, offer an ongoing and perceptible evaluation of natural circumstances, helping specialists screen and answer environmental changes.

2. Effects of Human Exercises
Human-initiated aggravations, like urbanization, deforestation, and environmental change, can fundamentally affect bird discussions. Expanded surrounding clamor levels, for example, may disrupt the capacity of birds to actually convey. Understanding the results of human exercises on bird correspondence is fundamental for creating protection systems that relieve adverse consequences and safeguard biodiversity.

Mechanical Advances and Future Headings
1. Acoustic Observing Organizations
The foundation of acoustic checking organizations, using an organization of decisively positioned receivers, permits scientists to screen bird discussions for a huge scope. These organizations empower the constant assortment of sound information, giving a thorough comprehension of avian vocalizations across various scenes and biological systems.

2. AI and Mechanized Investigation
Progresses in AI calculations have worked with robotized examination of enormous datasets, making it conceivable to productively distinguish and classify bird vocalizations more. These apparatuses speed up the handling of bioacoustic information, empowering analysts to zero in on deciphering the natural and social parts of bird discussions.

Chapter 6:
The Role of Environment in Communication

Correspondence is a basic part of human communication, filling in as the bedrock whereupon connections, social orders, and societies are fabricated. While verbal and non-verbal signals assume essential parts in passing on messages, the climate in which correspondence happens fundamentally impacts the adequacy and subtleties of the message. The climate envelops the physical, social, social, and mental setting in which correspondence happens. This article investigates the multi-layered job of the climate in correspondence, digging into how different ecological elements shape and form the manner in which people trade data.

Actual Climate and Correspondence

The actual climate, comprising of the environmental elements and setting where correspondence happens, assumes a significant part in forming connections. For example, the design of a room, its lighting, temperature, and clamor levels can significantly influence the correspondence cycle. In a sufficiently bright and calm space, people might find it simpler to move and participate in significant discussions. Running against the norm, an uproarious and turbulent climate might upset viable correspondence, prompting errors and misinterpretations.

Besides, the actual distance between communicators, known as proxemics, is a crucial viewpoint impacted by the climate. Various societies have fluctuating standards in regards to individual space, and understanding these standards is vital for fruitful multifaceted correspondence. In a packed metropolitan setting, individuals might adjust to more modest individual space, while in country regions, people could favor more huge distances during discussions.

Natural factors additionally impact the decision of correspondence channels. In an up close and personal setting, non-verbal prompts like looks, motions, and non-verbal communication are promptly accessible, improving the correspondence experience. Notwithstanding, in a virtual climate, where people impart through screens and consoles, the shortfall of actual presence can change the elements of correspondence. Understanding the effect of the actual climate permits people to adjust their correspondence methodologies to upgrade viability.

Social Climate and Correspondence

The social climate incorporates the cultural and relational elements that shape correspondence. Social designs, orders, and power elements impact how people communicate their thoughts and decipher messages. In a work environment, for instance, the progressive design can influence the progression of data. Subordinates might wonder whether or not to discuss transparently with bosses, dreading repercussions, which can block the free trade of thoughts.

Social standards and values are basic parts of the social climate, significantly affecting correspondence styles. High-setting societies, like those in numerous Asian nations, depend on verifiable and non-verbal correspondence, though low-setting societies, similar to those in Western social orders, stress unequivocal verbal articulation. Understanding these social distinctions is essential for successful intercultural correspondence, forestalling misconceptions and advancing common regard.

The social climate likewise incorporates virtual entertainment and computerized stages, which have changed the manner in which individuals convey. The ascent of virtual entertainment has worked with prompt correspondence on a worldwide scale, separating topographical hindrances. In any case, it has additionally presented new difficulties, like the spread of deception and the disintegration of eye to eye associations. The social climate's computerized viewpoints expect people to explore virtual spaces deliberately, taking into account the effect of their words and activities on a possibly tremendous and various crowd.

Mental Climate and Correspondence

People's psychological and profound states, involving the mental climate, essentially impact correspondence. Feelings like bliss, outrage, misery, or dread can variety the understanding of messages, prompting changing reactions. An individual in a positive profound state might be more open to data, while somebody encountering pressure or uneasiness could battle to understand or answer successfully.

Additionally, individual contrasts in character, mental styles, and correspondence inclinations add to the mental climate. Contemplative people, for example, may favor composed correspondence or more modest social scenes, while social butterflies might flourish in bigger parties and up close and personal connections. Perceiving and regarding these distinctions is fundamental for cultivating comprehensive and powerful correspondence.

The mental climate likewise includes the impact of previous encounters, injuries, and social molding on correspondence. People with various valuable encounters might decipher a similar message in an unexpected way, and recognizing these distinctions is pivotal for keeping away from accidental contentions.

Furthermore, the mental effect of correspondence can't be undervalued, as words have the ability to move, propel, hurt, or recuperate. Establishing a positive and strong mental climate is fundamental for supporting sound connections and successful correspondence.

Ecological Variation and Correspondence Ability
Correspondence capability, the capacity to actually pass on and decipher messages in different settings, expects people to handily adjust to various conditions. Adjusting to the actual climate includes picking suitable correspondence channels, taking into account proxemics, and overseeing outer interruptions. In the social climate, people should explore power elements, social contrasts, and advanced stages with responsiveness and social knowledge. Understanding the mental climate involves perceiving and dealing with one's feelings, as well as relating to others' points of view.
Variation to the climate is certainly not a one-size-fits-all cycle; it requires a nuanced comprehension of the particular setting and the people in question. Correspondence capability is a powerful expertise that develops as people experience new conditions and different correspondence challenges. Consistent learning, social mindfulness, and a readiness to embrace different correspondence styles add to creating correspondence skill.

6.1 Influence of Habitat on Communication Styles

Correspondence is a dynamic and complex cycle profoundly entwined with the climate where it happens. One frequently neglected part of this relationship is the impact of environment on correspondence styles. Territory, in this unique situation, alludes to the regular and constructed conditions that people occupy, enveloping geological areas, living spaces, and the more extensive biological systems that shape day to day existence. This exposition investigates the significant effect of natural surroundings on correspondence styles, digging into how the attributes of various territories shape the manners in which individuals articulate their thoughts, communicate, and construct connections.

Geological Natural surroundings and Correspondence
The geological territory, containing the regular scene and environment of a locale, assumes a critical part in forming correspondence styles. In districts with different geographies and environments, correspondence can be impacted by the actual difficulties presented by the climate. For instance, in hilly regions, where networks might be disconnected because of rough territory, correspondence styles might stress strength, independence, and a solid feeling of local area. Conversely, occupants of level, open scenes might foster correspondence styles that focus on perceivability, participation, and a more sweeping informal organization.

Besides, the accessibility of regular assets in a topographical territory can impact correspondence designs. Networks in asset rich regions might foster correspondence styles that reflect overflow, participation, and an emphasis on sharing data for common advantage. Conversely, those in asset scant conditions might embrace correspondence styles that focus on wariness, contest, and vital data the board to guarantee endurance. The geological environment additionally shapes social practices, and these practices, thus, impact correspondence styles. For instance, societies in waterfront regions could foster correspondence designs impacted by a dependence on fishing, with an accentuation on cooperation, shared liabilities, and liquid correspondence to explore the flightiness of the ocean. Understanding the harmonious connection between geological natural surroundings and social correspondence standards is fundamental for viable culturally diverse communications.

Metropolitan and Provincial Environments: Differentiations in Correspondence Styles

The qualification among metropolitan and provincial environments acquaints one more layer of intricacy with correspondence styles. Metropolitan conditions, portrayed by high populace thickness, variety, and quick moving ways of life, encourage correspondence styles that frequently focus on proficiency, curtness, and versatility. In metropolitan settings, people might depend on computerized correspondence stages, like messages and texting, to explore the requests of a clamoring and interconnected local area. Conversely, provincial territories, with their more slow speed of life and closer-sew networks, frequently develop correspondence styles that underscore eye to eye connections, narrating, and a solid oral custom. In provincial settings, where people might have further associations with their environmental elements and neighbors, correspondence is much of the time more private, considering itemized narrating and a dependence on non-verbal signs.

The fabricated climate of metropolitan living spaces, portrayed by high rises, public transportation, and computerized network, can shape correspondence styles to be more formal, succinct, and innovatively driven. The steady openness to a different scope of individuals and thoughts in metropolitan settings can likewise add to a more comprehensive and versatile correspondence style that obliges different viewpoints and social impacts.

On the other hand, the openness and quietness of provincial scenes can cultivate a more thoughtful and slow correspondence style. Up close and personal collaborations are esteemed in rustic networks, and correspondence frequently happens in common spaces, building up a feeling of shared character and common comprehension.

The normal environmental elements in rustic living spaces, like woods, farmlands, or mountains, may move similitudes and similarities that become imbued in the neighborhood correspondence style.

Computerized Living space: Virtual Conditions and Correspondence
The coming of the computerized age has acquainted another aspect with living space and its effect on correspondence styles. Virtual conditions, worked with by the web and advanced innovations, make territories that exist past actual limits. Online people group, web-based entertainment stages, and virtual work areas have their own one of a kind correspondence styles formed by the affordances and constraints of computerized cooperations.
In virtual environments, correspondence is much of the time text-based, depending on composed language, emoticons, and sight and sound components. This can prompt a democratization of correspondence, permitting people to put themselves out there in manners that might be not quite the same as up close and personal connections. In any case, the shortfall of non-verbal signals in virtual conditions can likewise prompt errors, expecting people to foster new relational abilities, remembering the translation of tone and setting for composed messages.

Computerized environments additionally offer namelessness and the capacity to arrange one's web-based character, affecting correspondence styles by empowering self-articulation and the investigation of assorted personas. Nonetheless, this opportunity can likewise prompt web-based disinhibition, where people might take part in correspondence that is more hasty or forceful than they would in up close and personal settings.
The worldwide reach of advanced environments takes into account diverse correspondence on an extraordinary scale. People from various topographical environments can associate, share thoughts, and team up on the web. Nonetheless, the test lies in exploring social subtleties, understanding assorted correspondence styles, and keeping away from misinterpretations that might emerge because of social contrasts.

Natural Promotion and Correspondence Styles
Environment impacts how people impart as well as the substance and objectives of their correspondence. Natural promotion, for example, is well established in the association among environments and correspondence styles. Activists and associations attempting to resolve natural issues frequently tailor their correspondence systems to reverberate with the particular attributes of the living spaces they try to secure or restore.

In natural surroundings confronting biological difficulties, correspondence styles might embrace earnestness, close to home allure, and a call to aggregate activity. Powerful ecological correspondence in these settings frequently includes narrating that features the effect of natural corruption on networks, untamed life, and environments. The objective is to rouse compassion, prepare backing, and cultivate a feeling of shared liability.

Conversely, living spaces with serious areas of strength for an ethos might observer correspondence styles that underline schooling, manageability, and cooperation. Messages in these settings might zero in on celebrating effective preservation endeavors, advancing eco-accommodating practices, and empowering long haul conduct change. The correspondence style lines up with the qualities and needs of the local area, cultivating a deep satisfaction and possession in natural stewardship.

6.2   Adaptations in Communication to Environmental Challenges

Correspondence is an essential part of human connection, significant for passing on data, building connections, and exploring the intricacies of society. Nonetheless, the viability of correspondence isn't just affected by human factors but at the same time is profoundly interlaced with the natural difficulties people face. This article investigates the variations in correspondence that arise in light of natural difficulties, analyzing how individuals alter their correspondence styles, channels, and methodologies to defeat hindrances presented by the physical, social, and mental climate.

Actual Ecological Difficulties and Correspondence Transformations

The actual climate, with its different scenes, atmospheric conditions, and geological highlights, presents exceptional difficulties to correspondence. In areas inclined to cataclysmic events like seismic tremors, storms, or fierce blazes, people have created explicit correspondence transformations to guarantee the security and prosperity of networks.

One key transformation is the foundation of early advance notice frameworks. These frameworks use different correspondence channels, including alarms, portable cautions, and public declarations, to scatter data about approaching natural dangers rapidly. The objective is to furnish people with ideal and exact data, permitting them to play it safe, empty if necessary, and limit the effect of the debacle.

In regions with outrageous weather patterns, for example, extreme winters or searing summers, people adjust their correspondence by integrating climate related language and similitudes into everyday discussions. This serves not just for the purpose of sharing data about the climate yet in addition as an approach to building a mutual perspective and a feeling of local area versatility even with testing weather conditions.

Besides, the actual climate can influence the accessibility and unwavering quality of conventional correspondence foundation, like power and web network. Accordingly, people group might foster elective correspondence systems, for example, the utilization of battery-fueled radios, local area release sheets, or verbal exchange correspondence organizations, guaranteeing that crucial data contacts people even without a trace of present day innovation.

Social Ecological Difficulties and Correspondence Transformations
The social climate, described by relational connections, social standards, and cultural designs, likewise presents difficulties that require correspondence variations. In people group confronting monetary difficulty, for instance, people might foster correspondence methodologies to address monetary requirements and advance asset sharing. This can include the production of local area organizations, trade frameworks, or the trading of data about work open doors and monetary help programs.
In areas with elevated degrees of social variety, people adjust their correspondence styles to explore etymological and social contrasts. Multilingual people group frequently foster a rich embroidery of correspondence works on, integrating code-exchanging, interpretation administrations, and social aversion to guarantee powerful correspondence across different gatherings. This versatility is significant for encouraging inclusivity and social attachment.

Additionally, social difficulties connected with disparity, separation, or social distress can prompt the rise of correspondence transformations focused on promotion and social change. Activists and underestimated networks might utilize stages like web-based entertainment, grassroots missions, and public exhibits to intensify their voices, share their encounters, and assemble support for civil rights goals.
The job of the nuclear family is focal in tending to social difficulties, and correspondence inside families frequently adjusts to offer profound help, share methods for dealing with hardship or stress, and reinforce familial bonds notwithstanding misfortune. Open and straightforward correspondence turns into a device for flexibility, assisting families with exploring difficulties all in all.

Mental Ecological Difficulties and Correspondence Variations
The mental climate, formed by individual feelings, psychological well-being, and mental cycles, acquaints one more layer of intricacy with correspondence variations. In the midst of emergency, people frequently experience uplifted pressure, uneasiness, or sadness, requiring variations in correspondence to offer profound help and advance prosperity.

One variation includes the development of compassionate relational abilities. People figure out how to listen effectively, approve feelings, and deal support without judgment. This type of correspondence is fundamental for establishing a steady mental climate, cultivating flexibility, and empowering people to straightforwardly communicate their sentiments.

In emotional wellness settings, where people might confront mental difficulties, for example, discouragement or injury, restorative correspondence turns into a significant transformation. Psychological wellness experts utilize procedures that focus on trust-building, compassion, and undivided attention to work with recuperating and recuperation. Furthermore, people might take part in self-revelation and look for help from peer organizations, involving correspondence as a device for destigmatization and local area building.

The mental difficulties related with vulnerability and vagueness, for example, those in the midst of monetary downturn or worldwide pandemics, lead to correspondence transformations pointed toward giving clearness and lessening uneasiness. Pioneers and associations might focus on straightforward correspondence, giving normal updates, clear rules, and exact data to assist people with settling on informed choices and adapt to vulnerability.

Mechanical Developments as Correspondence Variations

Despite natural difficulties, mechanical developments assume a urgent part in forming correspondence variations. The approach of the web, online entertainment, and computerized stages has reformed the manner in which people access and offer data. During natural emergencies, these advances become fundamental devices for correspondence, empowering continuous updates, far off coordinated effort, and the dispersal of basic data.

Virtual entertainment stages, specifically, have become strong specialized apparatuses during ecological difficulties. They work with the fast spread of data, assembly of assets, and the development of online networks zeroed in on common help and shared encounters. Hashtags, moving subjects, and viral substance enhance significant messages, empowering people to associate across geological limits and take part in aggregate endeavors.

Media transmission innovations, including video conferencing and texting, have become irreplaceable for keeping up with correspondence during circumstances that limit actual communications, like the Coronavirus pandemic. Remote work, virtual training, and telehealth administrations have become pervasive, displaying the versatility of correspondence because of natural difficulties.

Furthermore, the improvement of portable applications for catastrophe readiness, crisis reaction, and local area commitment represents how innovation can be saddled to address explicit ecological difficulties. These applications give continuous data about clearing courses, crisis safe houses, and clinical assets, enabling people to settle on informed choices during emergencies.

6.3   Impact of Climate and Seasonal Changes on Bird Communication

Birds, with their different and unpredictable vocalizations, participate in modern correspondence that serves different capabilities, including mate fascination, region foundation, and cautioning of likely dangers. The effect of environment and occasional changes on bird correspondence is a captivating part of avian way of behaving. Changes in temperature, precipitation, and sunshine hours can essentially impact the manners by which birds convey. This exposition investigates the unpredictable connection between environment, occasional varieties, and bird correspondence, revealing insight into how ecological elements shape the vocal ways of behaving of these noteworthy animals.

The Job of Tune in Bird Correspondence

Birds are prestigious for their tunes, which are intricate vocalizations that fill different open needs. One essential capability of bird melodies is mate fascination. During the reproducing season, male birds frequently sing to lay out and protect regions, drawing in expected mates with their unmistakable tunes. The quality and intricacy of a bird's melody can pass on data about its hereditary wellness and by and large wellbeing. One more urgent capability of bird tunes is regional correspondence. By singing, birds signal the limits of their regions and caution adjoining people to remain away. Regional questions are much of the time settled through vocal communications, limiting actual showdowns and rationing energy for conceptive exercises.

Moreover, birds use calls for different brief distance correspondence purposes, like making others aware of the presence of hunters, planning bunch exercises, or speaking with posterity. Bird correspondence, consequently, envelops a rich collection of vocalizations, each serving explicit environmental and social capabilities.

Environmental Change and Modified Movement Examples

Environmental change, driven by an Earth-wide temperature boost and related ecological movements, significantly affects bird conduct, remembering adjustments for relocation designs. Many bird species depend on natural signs, like temperature and day length, to decide the planning of their relocations.

As environmental change disturbs these prompts, birds might confront difficulties in synchronizing their developments with ideal natural circumstances.

One effect of changed relocation designs is the expected confuse between the appearance of transitory birds and the accessibility of fundamental assets, like food and settling destinations. This can impact the power and timing of vocalizations related with regional guard and mate fascination. Birds might have to change their correspondence procedures to adapt to changing biological elements.

Occasional Varieties and Reproducing Ways of behaving

Occasional changes, especially the progress among reproducing and non-rearing seasons, assume a significant part in molding bird correspondence. In mild areas, the reproducing season regularly corresponds with the appearance of spring, set apart by expanded light hours and hotter temperatures. These natural signals trigger hormonal changes in birds, impacting their conceptive ways of behaving, including vocalizations. During the reproducing season, male birds frequently strengthen their singing endeavors as they seek mates and lay out regions. The expanded vocal action draws in females and discourage rival guys. Interestingly, as the rearing season closes and birds enter the non-reproducing season, vocalizations might diminish as the center movements to scrounging and preservation of energy.

In tropical locales, where the differentiation between seasons might be less articulated, bird correspondence is much of the time impacted by different factors, for example, precipitation designs. A few animal types synchronize their rearing exercises with the accessibility of food assets, which can be impacted by the timing and length of blustery seasons.

Temperature, Moistness, and Vocalization Examples

Environment impacts the timing as well as the acoustic qualities of bird vocalizations. Temperature and moistness can influence the transmission of sound through the climate, affecting the reach and clearness of bird tunes. Hotter temperatures might improve sound transmission, permitting birds to impart over longer distances, while high stickiness can assimilate sound, restricting its engendering.

Birds might change their vocalization designs in light of ecological circumstances. For instance, in blistering and muggy circumstances, birds could change the recurrence or plentifulness of their calls to improve correspondence inside the requirements of the predominant climate. These transformations exhibit the adaptability of bird correspondence even with climatic varieties.

Influences on Tune Learning and Social Transmission
Many bird species gain their melodies from conspecifics, a cycle known as tune learning. Environment actuated modifications in the planning of rearing seasons and the accessibility of grown-up guides can affect the learning potential open doors for youthful birds. Changes in the construction of bird networks because of environment variances might prompt changes in the accessibility and variety of tune models, possibly impacting the social transmission of vocal collections.

Besides, adjustments in living space sythesis and asset accessibility, driven by environmental change, can impact the organization of bird networks. This might prompt changes in the acoustic climate, influencing the specific tensions on bird vocalizations. Thus, this can impact the advancement of tune qualities, adding to the unique idea of bird correspondence in light of natural difficulties.

Human-Initiated Ecological Changes
Notwithstanding regular environment varieties, human-prompted ecological changes can essentially affect bird correspondence. Urbanization, territory fracture, and commotion contamination related with human exercises can modify the acoustic scenes where birds impart. Metropolitan conditions, portrayed by consistent anthropogenic clamor, may present difficulties for birds that depend on acoustic signs for mate fascination and region guard.

Commotion contamination from metropolitan regions can disrupt the identification of unpretentious acoustic signs in bird melodies, possibly influencing mate determination and domain foundation. Some bird species, be that as it may, exhibit exceptional flexibility by changing the recurrence or timing of their vocalizations to limit the effect of human-produced clamor.

Preservation Suggestions
Understanding the effect of environment and ecological changes on bird correspondence has significant ramifications for preservation endeavors. Changes in relocation designs, reproducing ways of behaving, and vocalization examples can act as signs of more extensive environmental movements. Observing changes in bird correspondence can give significant bits of knowledge into the soundness of biological systems and the viability of protection measures.

Preservation techniques need to think about the unique idea of bird correspondence and its aversion to natural changes. Safeguarding and reestablishing natural surroundings, alleviating environmental change, and tending to human-initiated unsettling influences are fundamental for keeping up with the honesty of avian correspondence frameworks.

Preservationists can likewise utilize acoustic observing methods to survey bird populaces and track changes in vocalization designs after some time.

Chapter 7:
Human-Induced Changes in Avian Communication

Avian correspondence, the perplexing language of birds communicated through vocalizations, assumes a basic part in biological frameworks. Birds utilize different vocalizations for mate fascination, region safeguard, and route, adding to the rich woven artwork of regular sounds in their surroundings. Notwithstanding, the steady extension of human exercises has introduced phenomenal changes in these environments, applying huge effect on avian correspondence. This paper dives into the complex effect of human-prompted adjustments on the informative ways of behaving of birds, looking at the results of natural surroundings alterations, clamor contamination, light contamination, substance toxins, environmental change, and innovative advances.

II. Human-Incited Living space Changes

As urbanization infringes upon normal scenes, changing the actual texture of avian living spaces, birds wrestle with the difficulties of adjusting to these changed conditions. The broad reach of urban areas and the getting free from immense parcels of woods upset conventional settling and reproducing locales, constraining avian populaces to adjust to new circumstances. Moreover, deforestation, powered by human exercises, represents an immediate danger to transient examples and further strengthens the battle for reasonable favorable places. These territory adjustments reach out past actual changes to envelop shifts in the acoustic climate, affecting the actual embodiment of avian correspondence.

III. Commotion Contamination

A side-effect of urbanization and industrialization, commotion contamination has turned into an inescapable natural stressor with significant ramifications for avian correspondence. The regular orchestra of bird melodies is progressively overwhelmed by the racket of human exercises, as anthropogenic commotion impedes the sensitive acoustic subtleties indispensable for avian correspondence. Birds, dependent on vocalizations for mate determination, region foundation, and cautioning signals, face the test of adjusting to a hear-able scene generally modified by human presence. This part investigates the many-sided manners by which commotion contamination shapes avian correspondence, specifying the repercussions of concealing regular sounds and changing vocalization designs.

IV. Light Contamination

In the nighttime domains, where avian correspondence takes on an alternate aspect, the infringement of light contamination disturbs longstanding personal conduct standards. As metropolitan regions become on fire with counterfeit light, the regular patterns of haziness and light are darkened, influencing the circadian rhythms of both diurnal and nighttime birds. Nighttime species, especially, experience difficulties in exploring their surroundings and motioning toward likely mates in a world progressively enlightened by human exercises. This part tests into the outcomes of light contamination on avian correspondence, inspecting what adjusted lighting conditions mean for mating ceremonies and relocation.

V. Synthetic Contamination

The expansion of pesticides, modern poisons, and impurities in water sources represents a huge danger to avian populaces and their correspondence frameworks. Birds, as basic parts of environments, face the circuitous results of human-incited compound contamination. Pesticides, intended to safeguard crops, accidentally influence avian networks, prompting decreases in bug populaces that birds depend on for food. This part investigates the many-sided connections between compound poisons and avian correspondence, revealing insight into the flowing impacts of ecological foreign substances on bird species and their capacity to pass vital data on through vocalizations.

VI. Environmental Change

As an outcome of anthropogenic exercises, environmental change arises as an unavoidable power reshaping avian living spaces and relocation designs. Birds, finely sensitive to ecological prompts, wind up wrestling with modified rearing seasons, moving reaches, and flighty weather conditions. These progressions disturb laid out movement courses as well as require transformations in avian correspondence to adapt to the advancing environmental elements. This part dives into the multifaceted manners by which environmental change impacts avian correspondence, investigating the results of movements in reproducing and wintering ranges and the difficulties presented by outrageous climate occasions.

VII. Innovative Advances

Headways in innovation, while giving significant apparatuses to logical exploration, present the two open doors and difficulties for avian correspondence. Telemetry and following investigations offer exceptional bits of knowledge into movement designs, uncovering the complex subtleties of avian excursions across huge distances.

In any case, the unavoidable impact of innovation reaches out past observational advantages, affecting bird ways of behaving because of the always developing presence of human-made gadgets. This part analyzes the double job of mechanical advances in enhancing how we might interpret avian correspondence while presenting likely dangers to the regular ways of behaving of bird species.

VIII. Preservation Endeavors

Perceiving the earnestness of safeguarding avian correspondence despite human-actuated changes, protection endeavors arise as basic mediations. Living space reclamation and security become the dominant focal point, expecting to moderate the effects of urbanization and deforestation. Promotion and strategy drives look to address the main drivers of contamination, carrying out measures to lessen clamor, light, and substance poisons in avian living spaces. This part investigates the complex ways to deal with preservation, featuring the job of these endeavors in shielding avian correspondence and advancing economical concurrence.

IX. Future Possibilities

As human-incited changes continue and possibly raise, the eventual fate of avian correspondence stays dubious. This part thinks about the proceeded with effects of urbanization, contamination, and environmental change on avian natural surroundings and ways of behaving. Imaginative arrangements and advances, including those determined by interdisciplinary examination, arise as likely roads for alleviating the difficulties presented by human exercises. The significance of public mindfulness and training in cultivating an aggregate obligation to reasonable conjunction highlights the interconnectedness of human and avian networks.

7.1   Effects of Urbanization on Bird Communication

Urbanization, the fast development of urban areas and human foundation, has significant ramifications for regular biological systems and natural life. Birds, as vital parts of these biological systems, experience huge changes in their natural surroundings and ways of behaving because of urbanization. One area specifically compelling is the effect of urbanization on bird correspondence. Avian species, known for their different and unpredictable vocalizations, face exceptional difficulties in metropolitan conditions molded by commotion contamination, changed scenes, and other anthropogenic variables. This paper investigates the impacts of urbanization on bird correspondence, revealing insight into the intricacies of how metropolitan conditions shape the vocal ways of behaving of avian networks.

I. Presentation

Urbanization, described by the development and improvement of urban areas, is a predominant power forming the cutting edge scene. As urban communities extend, normal territories are changed into metropolitan conditions, affecting biodiversity and natural cycles. Birds, as exceptionally versatile and strong animals, go through tremendous changes because of urbanization. One critical part of their way of behaving that is impacted by urbanization is correspondence, a crucial component in avian cooperations. Understanding the impacts of urbanization on bird correspondence is pivotal for appreciating the more extensive natural results of human exercises.

II. Changed Acoustic Conditions

One of the essential results of urbanization for bird correspondence is the change of acoustic conditions. Metropolitan regions are portrayed by consistent human-created commotion, including traffic, development, and modern exercises. This commotion represents a critical test for birds that depend on vocalizations for different purposes, like mate fascination, region guard, and cautioning signals. The regular soundscape of birds is much of the time concealed by the noise of metropolitan life, affecting their capacity to successfully impart.

A. Concealing of Normal Sounds

The unavoidable commotion in metropolitan conditions veils the unpretentious sounds that are vital for avian correspondence. Bird tunes, which convey fundamental data about domain limits and regenerative wellness, might be muffled by the persistent murmur of metropolitan exercises. This covering impact can prompt misconceptions among birds, influencing their capacity to lay out and protect domains, draw in mates, and direction exercises inside gatherings.

B. Changes in Vocalization Examples

To adapt to the difficulties of commotion contamination, birds in metropolitan conditions might display changes in their vocalization designs. A few animal varieties might change the recurrence or sufficiency of their calls to be more discernible in boisterous circumstances. These changes, be that as it may, can have potentially negative results, as modified vocalizations might pass on various data or sign a change in the bird's way of behaving. Noticing these progressions gives experiences into how birds adjust their correspondence methodologies to explore the acoustic difficulties of metropolitan scenes.

III. Territory Fracture and Settling Difficulties

Urbanization frequently prompts territory discontinuity, where normal scenes are separated into more modest, disengaged patches. This fracture presents difficulties for bird species that depend on unambiguous living spaces for reproducing and settling.

The adjustment of scenes in metropolitan regions can impact the accessibility and appropriateness of settling destinations, affecting the conceptive progress of bird populaces.

A. Changes in Reproducing Ways of behaving

Metropolitan conditions might provoke changes in the reproducing ways of behaving of birds. The accessibility of appropriate settling locales, like trees, bushes, and open spaces, can impact the choice of rearing areas. A few animal groups might adjust to metropolitan designs, involving structures and edges alternative for regular settling locales. Others might battle to track down appropriate areas, prompting shifts in reproducing ways of behaving, adjusted settling achievement, and changes in populace elements.

B. Rivalry for Settling Destinations

The restricted accessibility of settling destinations in metropolitan regions can strengthen rivalry among bird species. This opposition might bring about clashes an over area and settling assets, impacting the recurrence and power of vocalizations. Expanded rivalry may likewise prompt changes in the organization of bird networks in metropolitan conditions, with specific species flourishing while others decline.

IV. Conduct Changes and Variations

Urbanization prompts a scope of conduct changes in birds, mirroring their endeavors to adjust to the difficulties presented by metropolitan conditions. These progressions stretch out to correspondence ways of behaving, impacting the timing, recurrence, and setting of vocalizations.

A. Changes in Day to day Movement Examples

Metropolitan conditions frequently show particular examples of human movement, with expanded commotion levels during the day and diminished action around evening time. Birds might change their everyday action examples to keep away from top commotion periods, influencing the planning of their vocalizations. Nighttime species, specifically, may confront difficulties in exploring the metropolitan soundscape, prompting changes in their circadian rhythms and vocalization designs.

B. Vocal Variations for Metropolitan Living

Certain bird species show exceptional variations in their vocalizations to adapt to metropolitan circumstances. Some might sing at higher frequencies to all the more likely enter the commotion, while others might alter the construction of their tunes to improve correspondence in metropolitan conditions.

These variations feature the adaptability and flexibility of birds despite urbanization, exhibiting their capacity to adjust correspondence methodologies to suit the requests of their evolving territories.

V. Human-Prompted Dangers

Metropolitan conditions present different risks for birds, and the collaborations with human foundation can adversely affect their correspondence ways of behaving. Crashes with structures, correspondence towers, and different designs, as well as openness to contaminations, present extra difficulties for avian networks in metropolitan regions.

A. Impacts and Correspondence Interruption

The commonness of tall structures and correspondence towers in metropolitan scenes builds the gamble of bird impacts. Birds might crash into structures during flight, prompting wounds or fatalities. Such episodes influence individual birds as well as disturb correspondence inside populaces, influencing the elements of gatherings and reproducing matches. Understanding the ramifications of these crashes is vital for creating techniques to alleviate their impacts on avian correspondence.

B. Contamination and Wellbeing Effects

Metropolitan conditions are frequently connected with expanded degrees of toxins, including air and light contamination. These toxins can antagonistically affect bird wellbeing, impacting their respiratory frameworks, regenerative achievement, and in general prosperity. The effects of contamination on bird correspondence are interconnected with more extensive natural outcomes, accentuating the requirement for thorough ways to deal with address the difficulties presented by urbanization.

VI. Protection Contemplations

Perceiving the diverse effects of urbanization on bird correspondence, preservation endeavors assume a urgent part in relieving these difficulties. Techniques pointed toward safeguarding and improving avian correspondence in metropolitan conditions include environment reclamation, the making of green spaces, and the execution of measures to diminish clamor and light contamination.

A. Territory Reclamation and Green Metropolitan Preparation

Endeavors to reestablish normal living spaces inside metropolitan scenes add to the making of appropriate conditions for bird correspondence. Green metropolitan preparation, consolidating parks, green rooftops, and other green spaces, gives chances to birds to find reasonable settling destinations, search for food, and participate in correspondence ways of behaving. Such drives benefit bird populaces as well as upgrade the general biodiversity of metropolitan biological systems.

B. Clamor and Light Decrease Measures

Tending to the difficulties of commotion and light contamination in metropolitan regions is vital for protecting avian correspondence. Carrying out measures like sound walls, green passageways, and guidelines to control commotion levels can add to a more helpful acoustic climate. Also, lessening superfluous fake lighting and carrying out bird-accommodating lighting plans assist with limiting disturbances to nighttime species and backing regular circadian rhythms.

VII. Future Points of view

As urbanization keeps on molding the scenes representing things to come, understanding the continuous and expected future impacts on bird correspondence stays a unique area of examination. The combination of innovation, resident science drives, and interdisciplinary methodologies will assume critical parts in propelling comprehension we might interpret avian ways of behaving in metropolitan conditions. Future examination ought to zero in on the drawn out results of urbanization, the adequacy of protection methodologies, and creative answers for advance supportable conjunction between metropolitan turns of events and avian networks.

7.2   Noise Pollution and its Impact on Vocalization

Commotion contamination, an inescapable result of urbanization and industrialization, has arisen as a huge ecological stressor with expansive impacts on untamed life. Among the different scope of living beings affected by commotion contamination, birds, famous for their perplexing vocalizations, face extraordinary difficulties in metropolitan conditions molded by anthropogenic clamor. This exposition investigates the multi-layered effect of clamor contamination on avian vocalization, digging into the intricacies of how unnecessary commotion adjusts the correspondence ways of behaving of birds and the biological results that follow.

I. Grasping Avian Vocalization:

To appreciate the effect of commotion contamination on avian correspondence, it is vital for first grasp the meaning of bird vocalization. Birdsong serves different capabilities significant for their endurance and multiplication, including mate fascination, region foundation, cautioning of hunters, and correspondence inside gatherings. The perplexing examples and tunes of bird vocalizations are formed by regular determination and assume an essential part in keeping up with the natural equilibrium of avian networks.

II. The Idea of Commotion Contamination:

Commotion contamination, characterized as undesirable or hurtful sound that slows down typical exercises, has turned into an undeniably pervasive part of metropolitan conditions.

It envelops different sources, including traffic commotion, modern hardware, development exercises, and human amusement. The nonstop murmur of metropolitan life makes a whirlwind that saturates regular natural surroundings, testing the sensitive equilibrium of acoustic correspondence in avian networks.

III. Veiling of Regular Sounds:
One of the essential impacts of clamor contamination on avian vocalization is the veiling of regular sounds. Birds depend on their vocalizations to pass on indispensable data, and the presence of consistent human-created commotion can muffle these inconspicuous acoustic signals. The covering impact impedes correspondence connected with mate determination, region guard, and coordination inside gatherings. As an outcome, birds might battle to send and get urgent data, prompting misconceptions and disturbances in their standards of conduct.

IV. Adjusted Vocalization Examples:
Because of the difficulties presented by commotion contamination, birds might display changes in their vocalization designs. A few animal categories might change the recurrence or sufficiency of their calls to be more discernible in uproarious circumstances. These variations, be that as it may, can have potentially negative results, as changed vocalizations might pass on various data or sign a change in the bird's way of behaving. Noticing these progressions gives bits of knowledge into how birds adjust their correspondence systems to explore the acoustic difficulties of clamor contaminated conditions.

V. Correspondence Breakdown and Conduct Outcomes:
The effect of commotion contamination on avian vocalization goes past simple adjustments in sound examples. Correspondence breakdowns because of clamor obstruction can have significant social ramifications for birds. Powerlessness to really pass or get data might lead on to regional debates, decreased reproducing achievement, and difficulties in scrounging and hunter aversion. The disturbance of correspondence inside gatherings can subvert the attachment of avian networks, influencing their capacity to flourish in metropolitan conditions.

VI. Impacts on Rearing Ways of behaving:
Avian vocalization assumes an essential part in mate fascination and romance ceremonies during the reproducing season. Clamor contamination can obstruct these significant ways of behaving, possibly influencing the rearing progress of bird populaces.

The adjusted acoustic scene might thwart the capacity of guys to draw in mates through their tunes, prompting changes in matching elements and possibly affecting hereditary variety inside populaces. Also, the veiling of romance signs might bring about decreased conceptive achievement, affecting the general wellbeing of avian networks.

VII. Influences an on Area Foundation:

Regional correspondence, communicated through vocalizations, is key for birds to lay out and protect their domains. Commotion contamination disturbs this basic part of avian way of behaving, as the ceaseless racket of metropolitan life can veil the nuanced regional calls of birds. The failure to successfully impart regional limits might prompt contentions among people and effect the general security of avian populaces. In metropolitan conditions where appropriate regions are restricted, the outcomes of upset regional correspondence can be especially extreme.

VIII. Stress and Physiological Reactions:

Commotion contamination isn't just a disruptor of avian vocalization yet additionally a stressor that can get physiological reactions in birds. The steady openness to commotion has been connected to raised pressure chemical levels, adjusted conceptive physiology, and compromised safe capability in birds. These physiological changes, set off by constant openness to commotion contamination, add to the more extensive effect on avian wellbeing and prosperity, underlining the interconnectedness of ecological stressors and correspondence interruptions.

IX. Suggestions for Environmental Collaborations:

The repercussions of clamor contamination on avian vocalization stretch out past individual birds to affect more extensive environmental communications. The breakdown of correspondence inside and between species can prompt changes in local area elements, impacting the dispersion and wealth of avian populaces. Changes in vocalization examples might influence hunter prey connections, plant-pollinator cooperations, and other environmental cycles, at last molding the design and working of whole biological systems.

X. Preservation Contemplations:

Perceiving the impeding impacts of clamor contamination on avian vocalization is essential for the advancement of compelling preservation systems. Protection endeavors ought to incorporate both the moderation of clamor contamination and the reclamation of acoustic conditions helpful for avian correspondence.

A. Alleviation Systems:
Execution of commotion hindrances and sound-engrossing materials in metropolitan regions.
Reception of sound decrease advancements in transportation and modern areas.
Guideline of commotion levels through metropolitan preparation and strategy drives.
Public mindfulness missions to advance dependable commotion rehearses.

B. Living space Reclamation:
Making of green spaces and natural life hallways to give shelter from commotion.
Rebuilding of regular territories inside metropolitan conditions.
Mix of acoustic contemplations in metropolitan wanting to save calm zones.
Safeguarding of biodiversity to help different avian networks.

C. Examination and Checking:
Proceeded with research on the particular effects of clamor contamination on various bird species.
Long haul checking of avian populaces to evaluate the adequacy of protection measures.
Reconciliation of resident science drives to accumulate information on avian vocalization and conduct.
Coordinated effort between scientists, progressives, and policymakers to address the interdisciplinary idea of clamor contamination influences.

XI. Future Viewpoints:
As urbanization keeps on forming the scenes representing things to come, the effect of commotion contamination on avian vocalization stays a powerful area of exploration. Progresses in innovation, including acoustic checking methods and remote detecting, offer new chances to concentrate on the complexities of avian correspondence in evolving conditions. Future examination ought to zero in on figuring out the combined impacts of commotion contamination, investigating the intuitive effects of numerous stressors, and creating imaginative answers for advance maintainable conjunction between human exercises and avian networks.

7.3 Conservation Implications for Wild Bird Communication
Wild bird correspondence, communicated through perplexing vocalizations and social presentations, assumes a significant part in keeping up with environmental equilibrium, guaranteeing regenerative achievement, and supporting generally speaking biodiversity. As human exercises progressively influence regular natural surroundings,
understanding the protection suggestions for wild bird correspondence becomes basic.

This article investigates the meaning of avian correspondence with regards to protection, looking at the difficulties looked by wild birds and proposing techniques to defend their vocal ways of behaving and natural jobs.

I. Significance of Bird Correspondence in Biological systems:
A. Natural Importance:
Wild bird correspondence is a foundation of biological system elements. Vocalizations serve works like mate fascination, region foundation, cautioning of hunters, and coordination inside gatherings. These open ways of behaving add to the guideline of populace sizes, foundation of domains, and help of agreeable exercises basic for endurance.

B. Biodiversity and Species Communications:
The rich variety of avian vocalizations mirrors the variety of bird species. Various species have advanced remarkable correspondence systems to possess explicit biological specialties. Associations between species, worked with by vocalizations, add to the unpredictable snare of connections that supports biodiversity. For instance, a few birds participate in mutualistic connections, where vocalizations act as signs for helpful searching or hunter cautions.

II. Protection Difficulties for Wild Bird Correspondence:
A. Territory Misfortune and Fracture:
The transformation of normal territories into metropolitan regions, agribusiness, and foundation projects brings about living space misfortune and discontinuity. This upsets the acoustic conditions wherein birds impart. Divided environments make it trying for birds to lay out regions, find appropriate settling locales, and keep up with associations inside populaces.

B. Clamor Contamination:
Urbanization and industrialization present clamor contamination, changing the acoustic scenes in which birds convey. Steady anthropogenic commotion can veil normal sounds, obstructing essential correspondence capabilities. Mate fascination, region safeguard, and cautioning signs might be compromised, prompting disturbances in reproducing ways of behaving and populace elements.

C. Environmental Change:
Changes in environment designs, driven by a worldwide temperature alteration, influence bird movement, rearing seasons, and the accessibility of assets. These modifications present difficulties to the timing and design of avian vocalizations.

Environment actuated shifts in living space appropriateness may likewise impact the creation of bird networks, influencing the elements of vocal cooperations.

D. Human-Instigated Perils:
Impacts with structures, correspondence pinnacles, and openness to poisons present extra dangers to avian correspondence. These dangers can bring about wounds, fatalities, and disturbances in the social designs of bird populaces. Tending to these difficulties is fundamental for protecting the respectability of wild bird correspondence.

III. Preservation Methodologies:
A. Environment Conservation and Rebuilding:
Safeguarded Regions: Laying out and keeping up with safeguarded regions to moderate normal territories pivotal for avian correspondence.
Hall Creation: Executing untamed life passageways to associate divided living spaces, working with development and correspondence between populaces.
Riparian Rebuilding: Zeroing in on the reclamation of riparian territories, which are basic for the overwhelming majority bird species, to guarantee the accessibility of appropriate conditions for correspondence.

B. Sound Decrease Measures:
Metropolitan Preparation: Consolidating sound decrease contemplations in metropolitan wanting to make calm zones and limit clamor influence on avian correspondence.
Mechanical Arrangements: Executing commotion boundaries, sound-engrossing materials, and creative advances to moderate clamor contamination in regions visited by birds.
Public Mindfulness: Bringing issues to light among the general population about the adverse impacts of commotion contamination on bird correspondence and supporting for dependable clamor rehearses.

C. Environment Versatile Preservation:
Versatile Administration: Carrying out versatile administration procedures to address the effects of environmental change on bird territories and movement designs.
Research Drives: Supporting exploration drives to comprehend what environmental change means for avian correspondence and incorporating discoveries into preservation arranging.
Worldwide Joint effort: Teaming up universally to address worldwide environment difficulties and carry out protection estimates that think about the interconnected idea of bird species.

D. Alleviation of Human-Prompted Perils:
Building Configuration: Consolidating bird-accommodating plans in structures and correspondence pinnacles to diminish impact gambles.
Contamination Control: Carrying out and implementing contamination control measures to limit the openness of birds to destructive foreign substances.
Resident Science: Connecting with resident science drives to screen and report bird crashes, contributing important information for peril relief.

IV. The Job of Resident Science in Protection:
Resident science assumes a urgent part in checking avian correspondence and adding to preservation endeavors. Drawing in general society in information assortment and perception encourages a feeling of divided liability and fortifies the association among networks and their nearby biological systems. Stages that urge resident researchers to record bird vocalizations, screen conduct, and report surprising examples give important bits of knowledge to specialists and protectionists.

V. Future Headings and Exploration Needs:
A. Long haul Checking:
Laying out long haul checking projects to follow changes in avian correspondence designs and survey the adequacy of protection measures.
Integrating acoustic checking into biodiversity observing drives to catch the subtleties of vocal associations among bird species.

B. Interdisciplinary Exploration:
Empowering interdisciplinary examination that thinks about the crossing points between ornithology, nature, acoustics, and preservation science.
Examining the total effects of various stressors, like environment misfortune, commotion contamination, and environmental change, on avian correspondence.

C. Innovative Headways:
Utilizing innovative headways, including AI and mechanized acoustic observing, to upgrade the effectiveness and extent of avian correspondence research.
Creating imaginative instruments and applications that permit resident researchers to effectively add to avian correspondence research.

Chapter 8:
Technological Advances in Studying Avian Communication

Avian correspondence, the mind boggling arrangement of signs, sounds, and ways of behaving utilized by birds to pass on data, has long captivated researchers and bird aficionados the same. The investigation of avian correspondence gives important experiences into the social construction, natural transformations, and developmental elements of bird species. Throughout the long term, mechanical progressions play had an essential impact in upgrading how we might interpret avian correspondence, permitting specialists to dig further into the intricacies of bird vocalizations, visual presentations, and other open ways of behaving. This article investigates the huge mechanical advances that have changed the field of avian correspondence research.

Bioacoustics and Computerized Sound Examination

Quite possibly of the main mechanical leap forward in concentrating on avian correspondence is the advancement of bioacoustics and mechanized sound examination. Bioacoustics includes the investigation of creature sounds to figure out their capabilities and hidden components. The utilization of particular amplifiers and recording hardware permits specialists to catch and dissect the perplexing vocalizations of birds in their normal living spaces.

Computerized sound investigation, controlled by cutting edge calculations and programming, has turned into a fundamental device for handling huge volumes of sound information proficiently. This innovation empowers specialists to distinguish and order various sorts of bird calls, tunes, and different vocalizations with a degree of accuracy and speed that was beforehand unreachable. Accordingly, researchers can concentrate on the fleeting examples, recurrence balance, and individual varieties in avian vocalizations, giving experiences into species-explicit correspondence systems.

Radio Telemetry and Global positioning frameworks

The appearance of radio telemetry has reformed the investigation of avian way of behaving and development. Radio transmitters joined to birds permit specialists to follow their developments progressively, giving essential data about searching way of behaving, movement examples, and regional elements. This innovation has been especially significant in grasping the job of vocalizations in mate fascination, domain protection, and other social cooperations.

Worldwide Situating Framework (GPS) innovation has additionally upgraded the precision and unwavering quality of bird global positioning frameworks. Scientists can now get exact data about the geological areas of individual birds, working with the planning of their spatial circulation and development designs. This has been instrumental in concentrating on the effect of ecological elements, for example, territory changes and environment variances, on avian correspondence and conduct.

Rapid Video Recording

The utilization of rapid video recording has opened new roads for concentrating on visual presentations and non-vocal correspondence in birds. Many bird species depend on complex visual signs, including romance showcases, plumage examples, and body developments, to pass data on to expected mates or adversaries. Fast cameras catch these quick and frequently unobtrusive ways of behaving, permitting scientists to dissect them exhaustively.

Slow-movement playback of high velocity video accounts empowers researchers to take apart the subtleties of avian visual correspondence, like the exact timing and succession of developments. This innovation has demonstrated important in revealing the nuances of romance ceremonies, regional presentations, and other outwardly interceded ways of behaving that are vital to avian correspondence.

Sub-atomic Methods and Hereditary Examination

Propels in sub-atomic methods and hereditary examination have given a more profound comprehension of the hereditary premise of avian correspondence. Scientists can now research the hereditary underpinnings of vocal learning, a peculiarity saw in specific bird species where people gain their melodies from conspecifics. By concentrating on the declaration of explicit qualities connected with vocalizations, researchers can unwind the atomic components that administer avian correspondence and add to how we might interpret its advancement.

Hereditary examination likewise permits specialists to investigate the heritability of correspondence attributes and research how particular tensions shape the variety of signs inside and between bird species. This interdisciplinary methodology, consolidating atomic science with conduct nature, has prompted pivotal revelations about the hereditary groundworks of avian correspondence and its part in speciation and transformation.

Neuroimaging and Mind Planning

Understanding the brain premise of avian correspondence has been enormously worked with by progressions in neuroimaging strategies and cerebrum planning.

Useful Attractive Reverberation Imaging (fMRI) and positron discharge tomography (PET) filters have been utilized to concentrate on the brain processes and cerebrum locales associated with vocal creation and discernment in birds.

By planning the mind movement related with various parts of avian correspondence, analysts gain bits of knowledge into the mental cycles hidden vocal learning, mimicry, and the translation of social signs. Near examinations across bird species with shifting correspondence procedures add to how we might interpret the development of brain circuits related with correspondence ways of behaving.

8.1 Overview of Modern Research Techniques

The scene of logical exploration has gone through a significant change in ongoing many years, driven by quick mechanical progressions. Current exploration strategies have sped up the speed of disclosure as well as extended the extension and profundity of examinations across different disciplines. This article gives a thorough outline of some key present day research procedures that are molding the manner in which researchers approach their work.

Genomic Sequencing and CRISPR-Cas9 Innovation

Perhaps of the most progressive improvement in atomic science is genomic sequencing, which includes deciding the total DNA succession of an organic entity. This method has extensive ramifications for fields like hereditary qualities, medication, and developmental science. The Human Genome Undertaking, finished in 2003, denoted an achievement in genomic research, giving a reference to figuring out human hereditary qualities.

Besides, the approach of CRISPR-Cas9 innovation has upset hereditary altering. CRISPR (Bunched Consistently Interspaced Short Palindromic Rehashes) and Cas9 (CRISPR-related protein 9) permit researchers to definitively alter qualities by eliminating, adding, or modifying explicit DNA successions. This advancement has significant ramifications for hereditary exploration, offering the possibility to address hereditary problems and specialist organic entities for different purposes.

High level Imaging Procedures

Current exploration benefits altogether from cutting edge imaging methods that give remarkable goal and experiences into the tiny world. High-goal microscopy, for example, confocal and super-goal microscopy, empowers researchers to picture cell designs and dynamic cycles at the nanoscale. This has suggestions for grasping cell capabilities, infection systems, and medication improvement.

In the field of clinical imaging, methods like Attractive Reverberation Imaging (X-ray), Positron Outflow Tomography (PET), and registered tomography (CT) examines have become irreplaceable for harmless representation of inner designs in living creatures.

These imaging strategies add to clinical conclusion, treatment arranging, and checking illness movement.

Enormous Information Investigation and AI

The expansion of computerized information has led to the significance of huge information examination and AI in research. These strategies empower analysts to break down huge datasets, remove examples, and make forecasts. In fields like genomics, environment science, and sociologies, huge information examination works with the distinguishing proof of patterns and connections that may not be evident through customary strategies.

AI calculations, specifically, are being applied in different fields, from foreseeing illness episodes to enhancing producing processes. In logical exploration, AI is utilized for picture examination, information translation, and example acknowledgment, offering the possibility to smooth out investigation and uncover stowed away connections inside complex datasets.

Neuroimaging and Mind Availability Studies

Progressions in neuroimaging procedures have significantly improved how we might interpret the mind's design and capability. Practical Attractive Reverberation Imaging (fMRI) and electroencephalography (EEG) permit specialists to concentrate on cerebrum action continuously. This has significant ramifications for neuroscience, brain research, and mental science, empowering researchers to explore brain processes related with discernment, insight, and conduct.

Mind availability studies, worked with by strategies like dissemination tensor imaging (DTI), shed light on the complex organizations of brain associations inside the cerebrum. Understanding how different cerebrum districts impart and connect adds as far as anyone is concerned of neurological problems, mental health, and the brain premise of complicated ways of behaving.

Ecological Observing and Remote Detecting

Mechanical advancements have changed the manner in which analysts screen and study the climate. Remote detecting innovations, including satellite symbolism and automated elevated vehicles (UAVs), give a 10,000 foot perspective of the World's surface. These apparatuses are fundamental for checking environmental change, evaluating land use examples, and concentrating on cataclysmic events.

Ecological sensors, conveyed in different environments, consistently gather information on variables like temperature, moistness, and contamination levels. This constant natural checking adds to how we might interpret environmental cycles, biodiversity elements, and the effect of human exercises in the world.

Quantum Registering
In the domain of computational exploration, quantum figuring addresses a change in outlook. Conventional PCs use pieces to handle data, addressing either a 0 or a 1. Quantum PCs, then again, use qubits, which can exist in different states at the same time because of the standards of quantum superposition and entrapment. This permits quantum PCs to perform complex estimations at speeds impossible with old style PCs. While quantum processing is still in its earliest stages, it holds huge commitment for taking care of perplexing issues in fields like cryptography, streamlining, and drug disclosure. As the innovation develops, quantum PCs are supposed to reform computational ways to deal with logical exploration.

Web-based Entertainment and Computerized Ethnography
The coming of virtual entertainment has changed the manner in which scientists concentrate on human way of behaving and social elements. Advanced ethnography includes the examination of online networks, connections, and correspondence designs. Specialists can acquire bits of knowledge into social peculiarities, political patterns, and popular sentiments overwhelmingly of information created via online entertainment stages.
The reconciliation of web-based entertainment information with customary ethnographic techniques gives a more exhaustive comprehension of contemporary social orders. Analysts can investigate how people and networks communicate their thoughts, structure associations, and explore the advanced scene, offering significant viewpoints on the crossing point of innovation and culture.

8.2   Advancements in Bioacoustics and Tracking Technologies
The investigation of creature conduct, especially in the domain of bioacoustics and following advancements, has gone through an extraordinary development lately. Bioacoustics, the discipline that spotlights on the investigation of creature sounds for grasping correspondence and conduct, and following innovations that empower observing of creature developments, have seen huge headways. These advancements not just improve how we might interpret the regular world yet additionally have reasonable applications in protection, biology, and untamed life the executives.

Bioacoustics: Disclosing the Ensemble of Nature
Bioacoustics assumes a pivotal part in translating the perplexing language of the set of all animals. From bugs to marine warm blooded creatures, every species utilizes an extraordinary cluster of sounds for correspondence, route, and conceptive purposes. Mechanical advances in bioacoustics have upset the manner in which analysts catch, dissect, and decipher these acoustic signs.

High-Loyalty Recording Gear:
Current bioacoustic concentrates on benefit from high-loyalty recording hardware that can catch an expansive scope of frequencies with extraordinary lucidity. Directional receivers, allegorical reflectors, and hydrophones intended for submerged recording empower researchers to gather itemized acoustic information in different conditions. This great hardware is fundamental for translating unobtrusive subtleties in creature calls and melodies.

Robotized Sound Investigation:
Maybe one of the most significant headways in bioacoustics is the improvement of mechanized sound examination devices. Strong calculations can now process enormous datasets, consequently distinguishing and ordering different creature vocalizations. This speeds up the investigation cycle as well as empowers specialists to reveal examples, varieties, and patterns inside the intricate acoustic collection of different species.

AI in Bioacoustics:
The joining of AI strategies further upgrades the capacities of bioacoustic research. AI calculations can be prepared to perceive explicit creature calls, even within the sight of foundation clamor. This innovation works with the recognizable proof of individual species, assessment of populace sizes, and observing of social changes over the long run, adding to how we might interpret biological elements.

Acoustic Labeling:
Acoustic labeling includes appending little gadgets to creatures that emanate special sound marks. These labels, frequently connected to people or delivered into the climate, permit analysts to follow the development and conduct of creatures overstretched periods. Acoustic labels have been instrumental in concentrating on transient examples, rummaging conduct, and social cooperations in sea-going conditions.

Following Advancements: Exploring the Undetectable Ways
Following advancements have developed to give specialists uncommon experiences into the developments and ways of behaving of creatures in their regular territories. These innovations improve how we might interpret untamed life nature as well as illuminate protection techniques and the board choices.

Radio Telemetry:
Radio telemetry has been a foundation of natural life following for quite a long time. This method includes appending radio transmitters to creatures and utilizing beneficiaries to locate their positions.

While conventional, radio telemetry stays a solid technique for concentrating on the spatial nature of many species, from little vertebrates to enormous hunters.

GPS Following:
The reconciliation of Worldwide Situating Framework (GPS) innovation has reformed untamed life following. GPS beacons give exact area information, permitting specialists to screen creature developments progressively. This innovation has been especially persuasive in concentrating on enormous well evolved creatures, birds, and marine species, giving important data about movement courses, home reaches, and environment inclinations.

Satellite Following:
For species that cover tremendous distances or possess remote and difficult to reach districts, satellite following offers an unrivaled arrangement. Satellite transmitters, frequently sun based fueled, give consistent following information, empowering scientists to screen the significant distance developments of birds, ocean turtles, and marine well evolved creatures. Satellite following adds to how we might interpret worldwide relocation designs and the protection of boundless species.

Biologging and Sensor Advancements:
Biologging includes outfitting creatures with information lumberjacks or sensors that record different boundaries, including temperature, profundity, and speed increase. This abundance of data gives bits of knowledge into the natural circumstances experienced by creatures and their reactions to these circumstances. Scaled down sensor advances have extended the potential outcomes of biologging, permitting analysts to accumulate itemized data without altogether affecting the review subjects.

Cooperative energies and Future Bearings:
The joining of bioacoustics and following innovations offers a synergistic way to deal with concentrating on creature conduct. Joining acoustic information with development designs gives a more exhaustive comprehension of the environmental jobs, social designs, and correspondence systems of species. This interdisciplinary methodology has viable applications in preservation, where informed administration choices depend on a comprehensive comprehension of untamed life elements.
As these innovations keep on propelling, specialists can anticipate significantly more modern and coordinated ways to deal with concentrating on the regular world. The cooperative energy of bioacoustics and following innovations holds extraordinary commitment for disentangling the secrets of creature conduct, adding to biodiversity protection, and cultivating a more profound appreciation for the rich embroidery of life on The planet.

As we explore the undetectable ways creatures navigate, these progressions carry us nearer to understanding and protecting the complex biological systems we share with the different species that possess our planet.

8.3   Insights Gained from Technological Innovations

The tenacious walk of mechanical advancements has re-imagined the scene of human information, pushing the limits of what we can notice, measure, and appreciate. From the microcosms of atomic science to the cosmoses of astronomy, mechanical headways have unwound secrets, tested presumptions, and gave extraordinary experiences across assorted fields. This article digs into the groundbreaking bits of knowledge acquired from key mechanical developments, investigating how these headways have reshaped how we might interpret the world.

1. Genomic Sequencing: Translating the Outline of Life

The coming of genomic sequencing has been a turning point in natural exploration. This weighty innovation permits researchers to unravel the total DNA groupings of living beings, offering significant bits of knowledge into the hereditary underpinnings of life. The Human Genome Venture, finished in 2003, denoted a fantastic accomplishment in genomics, giving an extensive guide of the human genome.

Grasping Human Wellbeing and Sickness:

Genomic sequencing has upset medication by working with the recognizable proof of hereditary elements hidden sicknesses. The capacity to succession individual genomes has opened roads for customized medication, fitting medicines in view of a person's hereditary cosmetics. Bits of knowledge acquired from genomic studies have improved how we might interpret acquired messes, vulnerability to sicknesses, and the potential for designated treatments.

Developmental Science and Biodiversity:

Past human genomics, this innovation has changed how we might interpret developmental science and biodiversity. Similar genomics permits scientists to follow the developmental connections between species, uncovering the common hereditary legacy that interfaces generally living life forms. Genomic experiences give a more profound comprehension of the systems driving development and the striking variety of life on The planet.

2. Environment Demonstrating and Earth Perception

Mechanical developments in environment displaying and Earth perception have been instrumental in concentrating on the mind boggling elements of our planet's environment framework. These headways not just add to how we might interpret environmental change yet in addition illuminate methodologies for alleviation and transformation.

Satellite Innovation and Remote Detecting:
Satellite innovation has changed our capacity to screen the World's environment on a worldwide scale. Remote detecting satellites catch information on temperature, precipitation, ocean level, and climatic structure, giving an extensive perspective on ecological changes. Experiences acquired from satellite perceptions add to environment demonstrating, empowering researchers to evaluate the effects of human exercises on the World's environment.

Environment Demonstrating and Forecasts:
Elite execution figuring has worked with the advancement of modern environment models that reenact the communications between the air, seas, and land. These models assist with anticipating future environment situations, permitting policymakers to pursue informed choices on environmental change alleviation and variation. Experiences acquired from environment demonstrating feature the earnestness of tending to anthropogenic impacts on the environment and give an establishment to creating maintainable procedures.

3. High-Goal Imaging in Medication
The field of clinical imaging has seen noteworthy headways in high-goal imaging advancements, changing diagnostics, treatment arranging, and careful mediations. These developments offer uncommon lucidity in envisioning interior designs and neurotic circumstances.

Attractive Reverberation Imaging (X-ray):
X-ray innovation uses strong attractive fields and radio waves to create nitty gritty pictures of the body's inward designs. High-goal X-ray considers painless assessment of delicate tissues, making it a priceless apparatus in diagnosing conditions like growths, neurological problems, and outer muscle wounds. Experiences acquired from high-goal imaging upgrade the accuracy of clinical analyses and illuminate designated treatment draws near.

Registered Tomography (CT) Outputs:
CT filters utilize X-beams to make cross-sectional pictures of the body, giving three-layered reproductions of inward designs. Propels in CT imaging, for example, double energy CT and iterative reproduction strategies, upgrade picture quality and decrease radiation openness.

Bits of knowledge acquired from CT filters help in the early identification of sicknesses, guide careful preparation, and add to headways in interventional radiology.

4. Quantum Processing: Releasing Remarkable Computational Power

The rise of quantum figuring addresses a change in outlook in the realm of data handling. Not at all like old style PCs that utilization pieces to address either a 0 or a 1, quantum PCs use qubits, which can exist in various states at the same time. This property, known as superposition, empowers quantum PCs to perform complex estimations at speeds impossible with traditional PCs.

Advancement and Complex Critical thinking:

Quantum PCs succeed at taking care of streamlining issues and complex numerical conditions that are computationally serious for traditional PCs. This ability has applications in fields like cryptography, planned operations, and medication revelation. Bits of knowledge acquired from quantum registering can upset ventures by giving answers for issues that were once thought to be unrealistic.

Reenactment of Quantum Frameworks:

Quantum PCs are especially appropriate for recreating the way of behaving of quantum frameworks, an errand that outperforms the computational capacities of old style PCs. This has significant ramifications for understanding the way of behaving of issue at the quantum level, adding to headways in materials science, science, and physical science. Bits of knowledge acquired from reproducing quantum frameworks make ready for the advancement of new materials and innovations.

5. Man-made consciousness and AI

The incorporation of man-made brainpower (simulated intelligence) and AI (ML) has saturated assorted fields, from medical services and money to independent frameworks and logical exploration. These advances empower PCs to gain from information, recognize examples, and make expectations, opening new roads for experiences and revelations.

Clinical Analysis and Treatment Arranging:

Man-made intelligence and ML calculations examine immense datasets of clinical pictures, patient records, and hereditary data to aid clinical determination and treatment arranging. Experiences acquired from these innovations upgrade the precision of illness discovery, anticipate patient results, and suggest customized treatment methodologies. The capacity to process and decipher complex clinical information at phenomenal velocities changes medical services conveyance.

Logical Information Examination:
In logical exploration, artificial intelligence and ML are applied to break down huge datasets, recognize examples, and concentrate significant experiences. These advances have been instrumental in fields like astronomy, genomics, and ecological science. Experiences acquired from computer based intelligence and ML-driven examinations add to the disclosure of new peculiarities, the distinguishing proof of novel biomarkers, and the improvement of exploratory plans.

6. Advanced mechanics and Robotization in Industry
The coordination of advanced mechanics and robotization in modern cycles has smoothed out creation, upgraded accuracy, and further developed proficiency. These advancements give significant experiences into enhancing fabricating processes, guaranteeing item quality, and propelling the capacities of different businesses.

Accuracy Assembling and Quality Control:
Automated frameworks outfitted with cutting edge sensors and machine vision innovation add to accuracy assembling and quality control. Experiences acquired from mechanical robotization incorporate continuous observing of creation lines, discovery of imperfections, and streamlining of assembling boundaries. This prompts further developed item quality, diminished squander, and expanded efficiency in enterprises going from car to gadgets.

Independent Frameworks and Robots:
The utilization of independent frameworks, including drones and automated flying vehicles (UAVs), has upset ventures like agribusiness, coordinated operations, and foundation review. Experiences acquired from the organization of independent frameworks incorporate productive harvest checking, fast conveyance of merchandise, and practical foundation support. These advancements offer answers for difficulties in assorted areas, upgrading functional effectiveness and wellbeing.

Chapter 9
Conclusion

The excursion of human civilization has been set apart by an unquenchable mission for information and understanding, and at the core of this pursuit lies the groundbreaking impact of innovative headways. From the infinitesimal domains of genomics to the naturally visible territory of room investigation, the direction of our comprehension has been significantly molded by the instruments and developments we've formulated. As we consider the horde experiences acquired from these innovative wonders, it becomes clear that we stand at the crossing point of exceptional conceivable outcomes and difficulties, diagramming a course toward a future where the skylines of information keep on extending.

1. Unwinding the Code of Life: Genomic Bits of knowledge

The unraveling of the human genome remains as a demonstration of the momentous capacities of genomic sequencing innovations. The Human Genome Venture, a fantastic joint effort that spread over worldwide limits, uncovered the plan of our reality, uncovering the complexities of the hereditary code that underlies human existence. Experiences acquired from genomic sequencing have risen above the domains of medication, developmental science, and customized medical services.

In the field of medication, genomic experiences have reformed how we might interpret sicknesses, offering a brief look into the hereditary inclinations that impact individual wellbeing. The capacity to succession individual genomes has led to customized medication, where medicines are custom-made to the extraordinary hereditary cosmetics of every patient. This extraordinary methodology has suggestions for sickness avoidance, finding, and the improvement of designated treatments.

Past the human genome, similar genomics has advanced how we might interpret developmental connections and biodiversity. The common hereditary legacy that connects all living organic entities has been uncovered, giving a complete point of view on the interconnectedness of life on The planet. Genomic bits of knowledge add to how we might interpret the systems of development, variation, and the perplexing dance of qualities across different species.

2. Earth's Environment: Displaying, Noticing, and Adjusting

Progressions in environment demonstrating and Earth perception innovations have introduced another time of understanding the dynamic and interconnected frameworks that administer our planet's environment.

Remote detecting satellites, furnished with state of the art sensors, catch an abundance of information, permitting researchers to screen changes in temperature, ocean levels, and environmental creation. These bits of knowledge are basic for fathoming the mind boggling interaction of normal cycles and human-actuated effects on the World's environment.

Satellite innovation, combined with superior execution figuring, engages environment models to reenact complicated collaborations between the air, seas, and land. These models give a brief look into likely future situations, empowering policymakers to settle on informed conclusions about environmental change relief and variation. Bits of knowledge acquired from environment displaying feature the direness of tending to natural difficulties, encouraging reasonable practices, and relieving the effects of an evolving environment.

3. High-Goal Imaging in Medication: Looking into the Body's Embroidered artwork

The domain of clinical imaging has gone through an upset, with high-goal advances offering remarkable lucidity in envisioning the perplexing scenes of the human body. Attractive Reverberation Imaging (X-ray) and Registered Tomography (CT) filters have become key apparatuses in the determination and treatment of illnesses. Experiences acquired from these high-goal pictures add to exact clinical findings, guide careful mediations, and upgrade how we might interpret the intricacies of human life systems. X-ray innovation considers painless perception of delicate tissues, offering nitty gritty pictures of organs, joints, and neurological designs. This ability has changed indicative medication, empowering the early location of sicknesses and the checking of therapy reactions. CT examines, using X-beams to make definite cross-sectional pictures, give three-layered reproductions that guide in careful preparation and mediation.

4. Quantum Figuring: Opening Phenomenal Computational Outskirts

The coming of quantum figuring addresses a change in perspective in the domain of data handling. Quantum PCs, outfitting the standards of superposition and ensnarement, can possibly handle complex issues that surpass the computational limits of old style PCs. Bits of knowledge acquired from quantum processing reach out across different spaces, from cryptography and streamlining to the recreation of quantum frameworks.

Quantum PCs succeed in tackling advancement issues, offering answers for difficulties in coordinated operations, money, and medication disclosure. The capacity to reenact quantum frameworks at a degree of detail beforehand out of reach opens roads for figuring out the key idea of issue. Quantum registering addresses a jump in computational power as well as an entryway to investigating the wildernesses of quantum mechanics and opening additional opportunities in logical exploration and innovative development.

5. Man-made reasoning and AI: Gaining from Information

Man-made reasoning (simulated intelligence) and AI (ML) have penetrated basically every aspect of current life, changing the manner in which we process data and decide. These advancements, driven by modern calculations, gain from tremendous datasets, distinguish examples, and make forecasts. Experiences acquired from simulated intelligence and ML examinations add to fields as different as medical care, logical exploration, and money.

In the domain of medical services, computer based intelligence and ML calculations dissect clinical information to help with diagnostics, therapy arranging, and illness forecast. Bits of knowledge acquired from these advances upgrade the effectiveness and precision of clinical direction, furnishing clinicians with significant devices for working on persistent results. In logical examination, artificial intelligence and ML-driven examinations add to information understanding, design acknowledgment, and the disclosure of novel experiences inside complex datasets.

6. Advanced mechanics and Computerization: Changing Ventures

The joining of mechanical technology and mechanization has introduced another period of accuracy, proficiency, and wellbeing across different enterprises. From assembling cycles to planned operations and foundation upkeep, mechanical frameworks and independent innovations have reshaped the scene of industry. Bits of knowledge acquired from these mechanical developments reach out to accuracy producing, quality control, and the advancement of functional cycles.

Mechanical frameworks furnished with cutting edge sensors and machine vision innovation add to accuracy fabricating by observing creation lines, recognizing absconds, and guaranteeing item quality. Bits of knowledge acquired from mechanization advancements lead to further developed proficiency, diminished squander, and expanded efficiency in businesses going from car to hardware. Independent frameworks, including drones and automated vehicles, offer answers for difficulties in horticulture, observation, and foundation assessment.

Decision: Toward an Eventual fate of Unending Investigation

As we ponder the bits of knowledge acquired from these mechanical developments, it becomes obvious that we are on the cusp of another time of investigation and understanding. The skylines of information have extended dramatically, uncovering the complexities of life, the intricacies of our environment, and the tremendous capability of computational and logical capacities. Notwithstanding, with these disclosures come significant obligations.

The information acquired from innovative headways conveys the heaviness of moral contemplations, ecological stewardship, and a promise to inclusivity.

As we explore the strange regions representing things to come, we really should move toward the uses of these bits of knowledge with a feeling of obligation and a pledge to everyone's benefit.

The union of these mechanical progressions offers a comprehensive and interdisciplinary way to deal with critical thinking. Genomic bits of knowledge illuminate customized medication, environment models guide maintainable practices, and artificial intelligence driven investigations streamline modern cycles. The coordination of these innovations makes a collaboration that pushes us toward a future where the boondocks of information proceed to extend, and the limits between logical disciplines obscure.

In this fate of perpetual investigation, the experiences acquired from mechanical advancements become the establishment for tending to the stupendous difficulties within recent memory. Whether unwinding the secrets of the universe, figuring out the complexities of the human cerebrum, or moderating the effects of environmental change, innovation stays the impetus for human advancement. As we leave on this excursion of revelation, let us embrace the open doors, tackle the difficulties, and develop a common vision of a future where the quest for information has no limits.

9.1   Summarization of Key Findings

In the tremendous territory of mechanical advancement, key discoveries arise as directing guides, enlightening the unfamiliar domains of information. From genomics to environment displaying, high-goal imaging to quantum registering, and computerized reasoning to mechanical technology, the scene of revelation is set apart by groundbreaking experiences that reshape how we might interpret the world. This summation looks to distil and enlighten the fundamental disclosures gathered from these innovative boondocks, featuring their suggestions and the direction they set for what's in store.

1. Interpreting the Hereditary Plan: Genomic Bits of knowledge

The disentangling of the human genome through genomic sequencing remains as a demonstration of the surprising steps in sub-atomic science. The key finding lies in the significant comprehension acquired about the complicated code that administers life. From customized medication to transformative science, genomic experiences have penetrated assorted domains.

In customized medication, the capacity to succession individual genomes has prepared for custom-made medicines in light of hereditary cosmetics. The effect stretches out to illness counteraction, conclusion, and the improvement of designated treatments, introducing another time of medical care customization.

Relative genomics, then again, has offered a complete perspective on the interconnectedness of life. Bits of knowledge acquired from concentrating on the common hereditary legacy across species add to how we might interpret development, biodiversity, and the hidden instruments that shape the variety of life on The planet.

2. Earth's Environment Elements: Demonstrating and Perception

Progressions in environment demonstrating and Earth perception advances have given key discoveries essential to understanding and tending to the intricacies of our planet's environment framework. Through satellite innovation and elite execution processing, experiences into environmental change, its effects, and potential relief systems have come to the front.

Satellite innovation, outfitted with cutting edge sensors, catches an abundance of information adding to environment demonstrating. Remote detecting gives a complete perspective on changes in temperature, ocean levels, and air piece, framing the reason for informed dynamic in environment related strategies.

Environment models, driven by superior execution figuring, reproduce mind boggling cooperations between air, maritime, and earthbound parts. These recreations offer experiences into likely future situations, directing policymakers in creating procedures for environmental change relief and variation.

3. Accuracy Imaging in Medication: Picturing the Concealed

The advancement of high-goal imaging advancements in medication has yielded key discoveries that alter diagnostics and treatment. Attractive Reverberation Imaging (X-ray) and Registered Tomography (CT) checks have become crucial devices, offering remarkable clearness in envisioning inner designs and obsessive circumstances. X-ray innovation takes into consideration harmless perception of delicate tissues, upgrading indicative accuracy. The experiences acquired from high-goal pictures add to early illness recognition, treatment arranging, and observing helpful reactions. CT checks, offering point by point cross-sectional pictures, help in careful preparation, interventional radiology, and give three-layered recreations to complete clinical experiences.

4. Quantum Figuring: The Boondocks of Computational Power

Quantum figuring, a state of the art wilderness, has disclosed key discoveries that guarantee to change computational capacities. Through the standards of superposition and ensnarement, quantum PCs succeed at taking care of perplexing issues, offering bits of knowledge into enhancement, recreation of quantum frameworks, and remarkable computational power.

In streamlining, quantum PCs tackle issues considered computationally escalated for old style partners. This key tracking down opens roads for headways in strategies, cryptography, and medication revelation. Quantum reenactment, then again, gives bits of knowledge into the way of behaving of issue at the quantum level, with suggestions for materials science, science, and physical science.

5. Computerized reasoning and AI: Gaining from Information

Computerized reasoning (simulated intelligence) and AI (ML) have introduced another time of experiences got from information investigation. These innovations, driven by refined calculations, have applications going from medical services to logical examination, changing the manner in which we process data and simply decide.
In medical care, artificial intelligence and ML calculations break down tremendous clinical datasets, upgrading diagnostics, foreseeing patient results, and suggesting customized therapy systems. Logical exploration benefits from computer based intelligence and ML-driven investigations, adding to information understanding, design acknowledgment, and the disclosure of novel experiences inside complex datasets.

6. Mechanical technology and Mechanization: Changing Enterprises

The incorporation of mechanical technology and robotization advances has conveyed key discoveries that reclassify modern cycles, upgrading accuracy, productivity, and wellbeing. From accuracy assembling to independent frameworks, experiences acquired from these advances reach out to quality control, functional streamlining, and answers for difficulties in different businesses.
In accuracy fabricating, automated frameworks furnished with cutting edge sensors and machine vision add to quality control, guaranteeing item quality and limiting deformities. Independent frameworks, including drones and automated vehicles, offer arrangements in agribusiness, strategies, and foundation assessment, giving experiences into proficient harvest observing, quick conveyance, and financially savvy support.

Determination: Towards an Eventual fate of Interconnected Disclosure

As we distil these critical discoveries from the mechanical boondocks, a strong story arises — an account of interconnected revelation that traverses the domains of life sciences, ecological stewardship, medical services, calculation, information examination, and modern effectiveness. The ramifications of these experiences are expansive, rising above individual teaches and uniting into a comprehensive comprehension of the world.
The disentangling of the human genome enables customized medication, permitting medical care to be custom-made to the individual hereditary cosmetics. Environment demonstrating and Earth perception guide our reaction to natural difficulties, illuminating arrangements and techniques for reasonable living.

High-goal imaging innovations offer extraordinary perspectives into the human body, directing clinical experts and propelling medical care diagnostics.

Quantum registering opens computational potential outcomes that were once considered impossible, promising progressions in advancement, cryptography, and logical examination. Man-made brainpower and AI influence information driven bits of knowledge, changing medical services and logical disclosure. Mechanical technology and computerization reclassify modern cycles, upgrading productivity, accuracy, and security across assorted areas.

As we explore the future, these key discoveries go about as compass focuses, directing us towards a time of interconnected revelation. The combination of genomics, environment displaying, high-goal imaging, quantum processing, computer based intelligence, and mechanical technology means an aggregate walk toward a future where limits between disciplines obscure, and bits of knowledge acquired from one field illuminate and enhance revelations in another.

In this interconnected future, moral contemplations and mindful advancement become central. As innovation keeps on propelling, our obligation lies in outfitting these vital discoveries for everyone's benefit, cultivating feasible practices, and guaranteeing that the products of revelation are shared evenhandedly across social orders.

The excursion of mechanical revelation is a continuous story, with each key finding addressing an achievement as we continued looking for information. As we look forward, the mechanical scene guarantees proceeded with investigation, where the limits of what is conceivable are constantly pushed, and the bits of knowledge acquired from these boondocks keep on molding how we might interpret the world in significant and extraordinary ways.

9.2   Call to Action for Conservation Efforts

In a period characterized by remarkable mechanical headways and cultural advancement, the delicacy of our planet's environments is turning out to be progressively clear. The speed increase of environmental change, loss of biodiversity, and ecological corruption highlight the criticalness of aggregate activity to save and safeguard our normal world. This source of inspiration for preservation endeavors is a request for solidarity, mindfulness, and obligation to protect the sensitive equilibrium of nature for current and people in the future.

1. The Territory of Our Planet: Criticalness in Preservation

The world is at a basic point where the outcomes of human exercises on the climate are appearing in disturbing ways. Environmental change, driven by the collection of ozone harming substances, is causing climbing temperatures, outrageous climate occasions, and disturbances to biological systems. Biodiversity misfortune, advanced by environment obliteration, contamination, and overexploitation, undermines the perplexing snare of life that supports our planet.

2. The Job of Preservation: Saving Biodiversity and Environments

Protection endeavors are critical in tending to these ecological difficulties. Biodiversity, the assortment of life on The planet, isn't just a fundamental part of our normal legacy yet additionally a critical calculate the strength and steadiness of environments. Preservation is tied in with safeguarding and reestablishing biodiversity, saving territories, and guaranteeing the supportable utilization of regular assets.

It is similarly urgent to Save biological systems. Timberlands, seas, wetlands, and different biological systems offer indispensable types of assistance like carbon sequestration, water cleansing, and environment guideline. Protection endeavors mean to keep up with the wellbeing and usefulness of these environments, adding to the general prosperity of the planet.

3. The Source of inspiration: What can really be done?
A. Individual Obligation:

Decrease Carbon Impression: Embrace supportable practices in day to day existence, like diminishing energy utilization, utilizing public vehicle, and limiting waste. The aggregate effect of individual activities contributes essentially to moderating environmental change.

Support Feasible Items: Pick items that are reasonably obtained and created. From food to dress, supporting eco-accommodating and moral practices sends a strong message to enterprises about buyer inclinations.

Instruct and Promoter: Remain informed about natural issues and offer information with companions, family, and networks. Take part in discussions about the significance of preservation and promoter for strategies that focus on natural assurance.

B. Local area Commitment:
Take part in Neighborhood Protection Drives: Engage in local area based preservation projects. Plant trees, partake in ocean side clean-ups, and support nearby drives that mean to safeguard and reestablish normal environments.

Bring issues to light: Arrange and take part in mindfulness crusades inside your local area. Utilize web-based entertainment stages to share data about natural issues, preservation practices, and examples of overcoming adversity to rouse others.

Support Protection Associations: Contribute time, assets, or gifts to associations devoted to preservation endeavors. These associations assume a critical part in examination, promotion, and on-the-ground preservation projects.

C. Corporate and Industry Obligation:
Take on Economical Practices: Enterprises and businesses ought to focus on supportability in their activities. This incorporates lessening discharges, limiting waste, and taking on roundabout economy standards to guarantee mindful asset the board.

Put resources into Green Advances: Embrace and put resources into innovations that advance natural manageability. From sustainable power sources to eco-accommodating creation strategies, inventive advances can drive positive change.

Straightforwardness and Responsibility: Organizations ought to be straightforward about their ecological effect and take responsibility for their activities. This incorporates unveiling data about asset use, discharges, and endeavors toward preservation.

D. Administrative Activity:
Sanction and Reinforce Natural Strategies: States assume a focal part in molding strategies that influence the climate. Sanctioning and reinforcing of regulations connected with preservation, emanations decrease, and security of regular territories are vital.

Put resources into Preservation Drives: Apportion assets and subsidizing to help protection drives, research, and the execution of reasonable practices. Legislatures can cultivate organizations with NGOs, organizations, and networks to boost influence.

Worldwide Joint effort: Ecological issues rise above borders. States ought to effectively partake in worldwide coordinated efforts, arrangements, and settlements that expect to address worldwide difficulties, for example, environmental change and biodiversity misfortune.

4. Mechanical Advancement for Preservation
Bridling mechanical development is necessary to the progress of preservation endeavors. Arising innovations offer new apparatuses and approaches that can upgrade observing, research, and the execution of protection methodologies.

A. Satellite Innovation and Remote Detecting:
Environment Checking: Satellite innovation considers complete observing of biological systems, following changes in land cover, deforestation, and biodiversity. Remote detecting gives constant information that is important for preservation arranging.

Unlawful Logging and Poaching Counteraction: Satellite symbolism can be utilized to identify and forestall unlawful logging and poaching exercises. This innovation upgrades the capacity to screen safeguarded regions and answer quickly to dangers.

B. Information Examination and AI:
Biodiversity Preservation: AI calculations can dissect huge datasets to distinguish examples and patterns in biodiversity. This helps with understanding species appropriation, movement examples, and populace elements.

Prescient Examination for Protection Arranging: Information investigation can be utilized to anticipate ecological changes and their effect on environments. This data is significant for creating versatile protection techniques despite environmental change.

C. Blockchain Innovation:
Production network Straightforwardness: Blockchain innovation can be used to make straightforward stock chains, especially in businesses adding to deforestation and territory obliteration. This guarantees that items are obtained reasonably.

Untamed life Preservation: Blockchain can support untamed life protection by making secure information bases for following and checking imperiled species. This innovation helps battle unlawful natural life exchange and supports preservation endeavors.

Determination: An Aggregate Liability regarding People in the future
The source of inspiration for protection endeavors is an energizing sob for people, networks, companies, and legislatures to recognize the interconnectedness of our activities and the prosperity of our planet. Protection isn't just a moral obligation; it is a basic for the endurance and success of people in the future.
By embracing reasonable practices in our day to day routines, taking part in local area drives, requesting corporate obligation, and upholding for powerful legislative strategies, we add to an aggregate power for positive change. Mechanical development intensifies our effect, giving instruments to screen, investigate, and address natural difficulties with remarkable accuracy.

As we stand at the intersection of environmental strength and expected annihilation, the decisions today will resonate through time. The way of protection is a way of trust, versatility, and obligation. Together, let us leave on this excursion, perceiving that the safeguarding of our planet is certainly not a decision however an aggregate obligation to guarantee a flourishing, biodiverse, and reasonable world for a long time into the future.